# The Rabbi on the Mount

# The Rabbi on the Mount

*How Jesus' Judaism Clarifies*

*the Sermon on the Mount*

by Phil Weingart

Published by Philip K. Weingart using Amazon's Kindle Direct Publishing platform.

©2019 by Philip K. Weingart

Contacts should be directed to:

Phil Weingart
72 Main Street, Apartment 3
Wareham, MA 02571

philipweingart@yahoo.com

Author's web site: http://philweingart.net

ISBN: 9781097499014

Cover art ©2019 by Phil Weingart. The Hebrew characters in the background are the divine name, YHWH.

# Praise for

# The Rabbi on the Mount

"...a must-read for the rational Christian. It brings a level of understanding to Jesus's ministry on Earth that is not easy to obtain without having been steeped in Judaism and Jewish observance."

Henry Gernhardt, Teen Challenge Massachusetts, Brockton, MA

"...this book reads like a first-rate discipleship manual."

Eric Chabot, director of Ratio Christi at Ohio State University and Columbus State Community College, Midwest Representative for Christian Jewish Foundation Ministries.

"...author Phil Weingart offers us an old yet fresh way of reading and understanding this timeless sermon by Jesus."

Shawn White, Christian Apologist, founder and President of Smart Faith Conferences.

# Table of Contents

# Chapter 1: Confessions of a Christianized Jew

The Sermon on the Mount is a bit of a mystery.

We who love Jesus hold Him to be God Incarnate, the Master whom we are to obey and the Teacher whom we are to imitate. Even many non-Christians are willing to agree that He was one of the wisest men ever to grace humanity with His wisdom, and many Jews are inclined to think of Him as a great and wise Rabbi—and to blame the ensuing centuries of Christian persecution of the Jews on the Apostle Paul.

We would expect the Sermon on the Mount, then, being the longest unbroken teaching by Jesus that we have, to be a source of unquestionable, indispensable wisdom. Consistent with that, many of the greatest souls in Christendom, from Augustine to Luther to Bonhoeffer, have written works explaining Jesus' teaching in the Sermon on the Mount. And some historians, even some secular ones, argue that the Sermon on the Mount built the morality of Western Civilization.[1]

And yet, the Sermon on the Mount is not like any other sermon we've ever heard. Jesus did not announce His subject, present bullet points, supply illustrations, then summarize the lesson and sit down. To most of us, it looks as though Jesus wandered through a string of unrelated platitudes like a lazy river depositing bits of debris on the bank.

Worse, some of the debris looks to us like beer cans and old tires. Jesus used illustrations in the Sermon that we scramble to explain away because we can't imagine what He was thinking. "If your right eye causes you to sin, tear it out and throw it away."[2]

---

[1] Willard, Dallas, *The Divine Conspiracy*, Harper Collins Publishers, New York, 1997, p. 130-131.

[2] Matthew 5:29

Y'know, Jesus, I'm really serious about following You, but self-mutilation is a bit too far. "Do not resist the one who is evil."[3] I just spent ten years learning how to avoid becoming the victim of control freaks, and I will never go back to that nightmare. "Until heaven and earth pass away, not an iota, not a dot, will pass from the Law until all is accomplished."[4] But we are not under the Law anymore, right? You meant "before the Resurrection," right?

We come up with facile explanations for these and a dozen other problems with the Sermon on the Mount and repeat those explanations to each other as though we had discovered great wisdom, but it never really rings true. Much preaching and writing about the Sermon on the Mount is remarkably unhelpful, giving us nothing that genuinely improves our lives. In private moments we might wonder vaguely whether we're missing something, but we'll seldom admit that publicly.

Believers who have heard the words of the Sermon on the Mount all their lives take their strangeness in stride and ignore it. But the oddness of Jesus' unorthodox oratory, his exaggerated, abrupt illustrations and his apparently unconnected string of moral platitudes is right there on the page in black and white, staring at us, daring us to criticize and making us dance around it. We admire His greatness but often ignore, or worse, rewrite His instructions because we can't fathom what He meant. And then we force each other to do those things that we made up ourselves, imagining them to be laws that He laid down for us.

Is that really what God intended?

For quite a while I was happy to leave much of the Sermon on the Mount on the shelf in my mind as "Probably important but too hard to understand just now." Maybe God would do me a favor and explain it before I died. Maybe I'd ask about it when I arrived in heaven. Whatever.

---

[3] Matthew 5:39

[4] Matthew 5:18

And then, I had to prepare a sermon about it.

Not the whole Sermon on the Mount, mind you, or even the whole of the Beatitudes. It was just one line: "Blessed are the meek, for they shall inherit the earth."[5] I was one of five lay teachers that the pastor called on from time to time to deliver sermons, and when he decided to do a series on the Beatitudes he assigned one verse to each of us.

There are few things more uncomfortable to me than having to deliver a teaching on a subject I really don't understand, so I settled in for some serious prayer and preparation. My first question was the hardest, in my mind, because I'd never heard anybody even attempt to answer it: "Why Beatitudes? What the heck are those anyhow? Why begin a sermon with a list of reasons why people in poor circumstances are blessed, without explanation?"

God usually helps me when I have to prepare a talk, but that does not usually take the form of actual words in my head. So I was a little taken aback when I received an immediate answer to my question, which I had asked out loud. More surprising than the fact that I got an answer, though, was the answer I got:

"They're *b'rakhas*."[6]

I was raised in a Jewish home and attended synagogue regularly, so I knew what *b'rakhas* were. But I have to assume that a lot of

---

[5] Matthew 5:5

[6] That "kh" represents a scratching sound made in the back of the throat, like the sound that people make when they bring up mucous (sorry about that) or like the sound in the German language that appears at the end of the name "Dietrich." Most English-speaking writers use "ch" to represent that sound like the Germans do, but "ch" denotes several very different sounds in English—the affricative "ch" in "chew your cheese," the hard "k" in "a chorus of chords," and the softer "sh" in "Chicago machine"—so I prefer to use "kh" for the back-of-the-throat sound.

you reading this don't, so let me explain. I'll start with an illustration from the movies:

At the beginning of the movie *Schindler's List*, the audience sees a man's hand lighting a pair of candles during fifteen seconds of silence. Then a man's voice begins chanting a rough, simple melody in a foreign language. The audience sees a family standing around a table covered by a cloth and bearing candles and a covered tray, and discovers that the singer is a bearded older man at the table wearing a hat, presumably the father or perhaps the grandfather. Then the audience is looking at the table with candlesticks but no people and no tray while the chanting continues. A few, lonely bits of text announce the production company and the title of the film over the image of the bare table and glowing candles. The prayer ends, and the camera hovers over a single candle as the flame sputters out.

Gentiles viewing this sequence do not know exactly what it is but they know that they are watching some sort of Jewish prayer and may guess correctly that the language is Hebrew. Most of them will be vaguely intrigued and wonder what it means, but will let it pass as the movie goes on without explanation. They'll get the point: this is about Jews.

Jews watching this have a different experience. We know that we are watching the beginning of the *Shabbat* (Sabbath) service that occurs in every observant Jewish home every Friday night all over the world. Pretty quickly we recognize the words of the *Kiddush*, the blessing over the cup of wine, and we also might recognize that the singer is singing in an Old Country accent since a lot of us had older European Jews in our synagogues when we were growing up and they prayed with similar accents. Most of us will recall the melody we used to sing the *Kiddush* ourselves, which was probably different from the melody in the film. The familiar blessing might trigger some pleasant nostalgia.

Like the Gentiles, we're likely not to know the meanings of all the words being sung. Most American Jews can chant Hebrew but cannot translate much of it.

However, nearly all Jews can translate the words near the beginning and the end of the prayer: *Barukh atah adonai elohaynu melekh ha-olam.* "Blessed are you, Lord our God, king of the universe." If you know the phrase, you can go back and pick it out of the chant; parts of it occur three times in a prayer less than a minute long.

In fact, this phrase occurs in nearly every prayer in the written Jewish liturgy, often several times. It is the connective tissue of our liturgy. Whenever Jews pray, we bless God over and over. *Barukh atah, Adonai.* "Blessed are You, Lord." For everything. All the time. It's how Jews pray.

For a simple example, the short versions of the blessings at the beginning of the Sabbath meal go like this:

*Barukh atah Adonai Elohaynu melekh ha-olam asher kidishanu b'mitzvotav v'tzivanu lehadlik nehr shel Shabbat.*

Blessed are you, Lord, our God, king of the universe, who made us holy with His commandments and told us to light the Sabbath lights.

*Barukh atah Adonai Elohaynu melekh ha-olam boray p'ree ha-goffen.*

Blessed are you, Lord, our God, king of the universe, who has given us fruit from the vine.

*Barukh atah Adonai Elohaynu melekh ha-olam hamotzi lekhem mihn ha-aretz.*

Blessed are you, Lord, our God, king of the universe, who has given us bread from the earth.

Some blessings are short like these, and some are longer, but they all thank God for what He has done, what He has commanded us to do, and who He is. We call these sorts of prayers *b'rakhas*. *B'rakha* is a form of the opening word *barukh*, which means "blessed."

So what I had just heard from the Holy Spirit, if that's who it was, was that the Beatitudes were actually ordinary Jewish prayers—but with a small but crucial difference, which I'll discuss in a moment.

Forty years, I had been a Jew in a Gentile Christianity, but I had never imagined that possibility. I committed myself to Jesus at the age of eighteen and spent the next forty-plus years of my life working at becoming Christian and ignoring Jewish things. I knew that Jesus was a Jew but I thought that all the Judaism I knew dated from the Middle Ages or later, and I was not sure what Jesus' Judaism would have looked like. I thought my experience was mostly irrelevant.

After hearing from God in that unexpected fashion, I had to do a little research to verify that Jesus might have used the same sorts of prayers that I had used growing up in the synagogue. I discovered that it was not just possible but likely. The *Talmud*[7] suggests that the prayers of the Jewish liturgy were given to Moses but delivered to modern Jews by *Anshei Knesset Hagadolah*, "the Men of the Great Assembly" who met between 400 and 300 BCE.[8] The Great Assembly was a special and unusually large gathering of the Sanhedrin[9] convened by Ezra the

---

[7] I don't expect most of my readers to know what the *Talmud* is. I will explain in chapter three.

[8] "Moses received the *Torah* from Sinai and gave it over to Joshua. Joshua gave it over to the Elders, the Elders to the Prophets, and the Prophets gave it over to the Men of the Great Assembly." *Talmud*, Tractate *Avot* 1.1.

[9] "Sanhedrin" is an anglicized version of a Greek word meaning "assembly." The corresponding Hebrew word is "*Knesset*." The normal Sanhedrin, a gathering of the ruling Elders of Israel, was seventy men. The Great Assembly was one hundred twenty, "great" being a reference to its unusual size and

Priest (the same Ezra who wrote the book in the Bible bearing his name) to consider how Judaism was going to continue after building the second temple, in which the presence of God was not as clearly manifest as it had been in Solomon's temple. I asked four Rabbis selected more or less randomly on-line and all four confirmed it; the modern liturgy with its many repetitions of "Blessed are You, Lord" was probably written by the Men of the Great Assembly, three to four hundred years before Jesus ministered, and probably had been in use since their day.

Suddenly the Beatitudes made more sense to me. There was nothing unexpected about Jesus beginning a sermon with *b'rakhas*. Observant Jews do *b'rakhas* before...well, everything. None of Jesus' religiously-aware, Jewish *talmidim* (disciples or students) would have been surprised when Jesus began His teaching with some *b'rakhas*.

But they might have been surprised, maybe terribly surprised, at what Jesus included in His *b'rakhas*. In fact, I suspect that they spent the entire time that it took Him to deliver the eight Beatitudes scratching their heads or muttering to folks sitting next to them, wondering whether Jesus was committing blasphemy—and not even really hearing the conditions or the results that Jesus was reciting.

Why? He was using familiar form and language that they had always used to bless God. They blessed God using those words many times a day.

Only, Jesus was not blessing God, He was blessing *them*.

Jews might express how blessed somebody was for some particular action, or by some particular good fortune: "Blessed be Abram by God Most High..."[10] But to introduce an activity? In

---

likely also to the unusual importance of its subject. The modern, governing political assembly of the nation of Israel is also called the *Knesset* and consists of one hundred twenty members, mirroring the Great Assembly.

the place where one ordinarily blessed the Almighty? It was badly out of place.

Jesus knew exactly what He was doing and how they would react. The fact that He was blessing them like they were used to blessing God was at least part of the point that He was making. Jesus was informing His disciples that in some sense they were like God. He was elevating them. They were holy. They were heavenly—not in the future, but right there on the hillside, and not after perfection but just as they were: poor in spirit, hungry for righteousness, and the rest. And they really, deeply did not expect to hear that, not b'rakhas blessing ordinary mortals.

I saw that this connected directly with the very next thing Jesus said in the Sermon: "You are the salt of the earth." And the next: "You are the light of the world." Same message, repeated.

Then I saw why Jesus had to reassure them, after calling them holy and talking of them as though they were the focus of the entire world's attention, that he was not trying to unmake God's revelation to the Jews: "Do not think that I have come to abolish the Law or the Prophets..."[11] It was because His opening prayers, which sounded on the surface like ordinary opening prayers, at the same time conveyed a notion so utterly foreign to their religious training that He had to reassure them, "No, this is not a departure from what God has revealed. It's consistent with it. God's revelation will never pass away."

And I saw that He summarized the topic at the end of chapter 5: "You therefore must be perfect, as your heavenly Father is perfect."[12]

---

[10] Genesis 14:19b

[11] Matthew 5:17. Most interpreters seem to think that Jesus was talking about the Jewish Law. He wasn't, as I will explain in chapter three.

[12] Matthew 5:48

Suddenly, the Sermon on the Mount did not seem like a lazy river of platitudes anymore. The first chapter, at least, connected. "What do you know," I thought, "this really might be a sermon after all."

It took me forty years as a Christian to begin to find some of the answers to the nagging discomfort that I felt every time I read the Sermon on the Mount. When I began to find those answers, I discovered them among things that were available to the Church from the beginning but which the Church had deliberately rejected for almost two thousand years because it was competing with Judaism and often persecuting it rather than benefiting from it. And I discovered them among things that would have been available to me personally from my upbringing if I had looked into them, but which I had deliberately avoided, first because I was a child and lazy, and later because I was more interested in becoming a good Christian than in being what I was born to be, a good Jew.

Please don't think that I imagine myself to be the first Jew to discover familiar patterns in the gospels. I'm one of many, and I'll be citing some of those who beat me to it in my footnotes. But God is restoring the Church's connection to Judaism, and I'm honored to participate in that.

Also, please don't think that I expect this book to answer every mystery of the Sermon on the Mount. I'm not really even trying to explain the Sermon completely, just those places where Jesus' Judaism illuminates some part of it that we Westerners are apt to miss. There are plenty of statements in the Sermon on the Mount that I will skip entirely, and when I am finished there will still be plenty of mysteries to solve. Only, there will be fewer of them, because understanding Rabbi Jesus' Judaism and the Jewish expectations of His disciples really does unlock a lot of what Jesus actually meant—which is often not what we have taken Him to mean, and in some cases is nearly opposite what we thought He was saying. We have a little back-tracking to do.

## Another Pleasant Awakening

I didn't hate being Jewish during those forty-some years while I was working so hard at being Christian, I just considered it irrelevant. It didn't matter what any of us were before, I reasoned, because we're all made new in the Messiah, as Paul said in Galatians 3:28: "There is neither Jew nor Greek, there is neither slave nor free, there is no male and female, for you are all one in Christ Jesus." I somehow missed the point that the same passage says there's neither male nor female in Christ, but there were still plenty of instances where my gender was relevant and my male characteristics were useful.

It was helpful to know a little Hebrew to study the Old Testament. It was also occasionally helpful to have the Jewish liturgy in my background, like when I was reading Luke 18:10-14 and recognized Jesus' description of the Pharisee's prayer as the *Aleinu*,[13] the standard Jewish prayer that occurs at the end of the Friday night Sabbath service.

It was also a nuisance occasionally to have to listen patiently while some well-meaning Gentile gushed to me about how thrilled they were to meet a "completed Jew." Often they would proceed to describe excitedly how much they enjoyed the Messianic congregation that they visited from time to time, sure that I considered such a congregation the height of Jewish practice.[14] I would listen politely and leave quickly.

---

[13] The *Aleinu* is sung in Hebrew, but the beginning translates into English as follows: "It is for us to praise the Lord of all, to proclaim the greatness of the Creator of the universe, for He has not made us like the pagans of the world, nor placed us like the heathen tribes of the earth; He has not made our destiny as theirs, nor cast our lot with all their multitude." Rabbinical Assembly of America, *Sabbath and Festival Prayer Book*, 1946, p. 37. Jesus imputed to the Pharisees a superior attitude coloring the otherwise accurate description in the prayer, and described their attitude with exaggerated words.

[14] A Messianic congregation is a Christian church established by Jews who recognize Jesus as the Jewish Messiah. They incorporate American-Jewish verbiage into their worship service and often include parts of the standard

I did attend a Messianic congregation for about six months, when I first moved to Philadelphia in 1993. I had been a Christian about 20 years at that time, and unconsciously I was grieving the absence of the Jewish community from my life. My Gentile friends were neither stupid nor uneducated, but there is an intellectual intensity and wit in the Jewish community that expresses itself very differently from most other corners of the American culture, and I missed it. Six months among Jewish Christians in Philadelphia cured my longing; and then I moved on to an Evangelical church that was relationally healthier and better for my family. In general, though, I really didn't care a fig about Messianic Judaism.

It wasn't until the spring of 2013 that the Almighty acted to wake up Jewish Me. I was attending a Vineyard church in Massachusetts, the pastors of which were responsible in apostolic fashion for a handful of Vineyard churches that they and others had planted in Spain. They took trips to Spain from time to time to visit these churches, and I decided in 2013 to go with them once.

Few Americans are aware of the role that Spain played in the history of the Jewish people. It was a central role. For about eight hundred years covering the Middle Ages, Spain was the one place in Europe where Jews could live without significant persecution. They had to pay the "unbeliever" tax to the Muslim overlords, but aside from that they were allowed to live as they chose and to prosper. They even helped the Muslims run some of the cities.[15] This continued until the Spanish completed the *Reconquista* in the fifteenth century, finally driving the Muslim invaders completely out of the Iberian Peninsula.

---

Jewish *Torah* service as well. Those services are nearly always Protestant in theology and liturgy, and often Charismatic or neo-Charismatic in practice, but not always.

[15] *The Jewish Encyclopedia*, Vol. XI, 1906, p 485.

And then, in 1492, King Ferdinand and Queen Isabella expelled all the Jews from Spain, and the Portuguese followed suit two years later. It was a disaster and an enormous betrayal for the Jews of Spain. Because the edict came suddenly they were forced to leave most of their belongings behind or sell them at a loss, and many people died in the flood of exiles. The many Jews who converted to Christianity in order to avoid the edict were never trusted and became subject to the Inquisition, which began about the same time.

As a side note, a Spanish Christian told me that most Spanish surnames that end with "ez" were names adopted by Jews converting to avoid banishment; they were the names of professions, like "Baker," "Taylor," or "Hunter" in English. If this person was correct, any person from a Spanish-speaking culture with a name like "Valdez," "Gomez," or "Sanchez" is likely the descendant of Jewish *conversos* from the fifteenth century. That these names are so common is a reflection of just how many Jews were living in Spain at the time.

In addition to that, today nearly all the Jews in Africa and the Middle East, aside from those in Israel who emigrated from Europe after WWII, are descended from Spanish Jews. They are called "Sephardic Jews," a reference to the Hebrew name for Spain, *Sepharad*.

Jews were unwelcome in Spain for the next five hundred years. I don't think that it's a coincidence that Spain during that time became one of the most difficult places on planet Earth to plant a Christian church; I think that God takes the mistreatment of the Jews personally. Faithful or unfaithful, we are His people, and Jesus Himself is a Jew. "As you did it to one of the least of these, my brothers," said Jesus, "you did it to Me."[16] Any Middle Easterner would recognize that sentiment right away.

---

[16] Matthew 25:40. And yes, I do think that He meant "Jews." In verse 32 he talks of gathering "the nations" before Him. "Nations" and "Gentiles" are the same word in Hebrew, and the same concept. You can make what you like of

Things changed in 1992, exactly five hundred years after the expulsion of the Jews. In 1992, King Juan Carlos of Spain visited the only synagogue in Madrid and formally apologized to the Jews for the expulsion, calling it the worst thing that Spain had ever done as a nation. Then he traveled to the oldest synagogue in America, which is in Newport, RI, and again apologized there for the expulsion of the Jews from Spain. He made it clear: "We did wrong. We're sorry. Jews are welcome in Spain."

It was 1992 when a number of Protestant churches, including my current denomination, the Vineyard, decided that the time was ripe to start planting churches in Spain. Again, I don't consider that a coincidence; Spain repented and God opened the doors again. And it was about twenty years after that opening of the Spanish nation that I found myself preparing for a two-week missionary jaunt with Vineyard pastors.

The pastors, Don and Nancy Andreson, did not give me any specific tasks for the trip, but the Holy Spirit did. I was led to prepare a brief talk in Spanish explaining the Jews' history in Spain and thanking the Spanish believers for welcoming us back into their beautiful country. It ended with my blessing the congregation in Hebrew and Spanish (but shown here in transliterated Hebrew and English), using the priestly blessing that appears in Numbers 6:24-26:

> *Yivarekhekha adonai v'yishmarekha*
> *Ya-ayr adonai panav aylekha v'khunekha*
> *Yisah adonai panav aylekha v'yasayn l'kha shalom*

The Lord bless you and keep you
The Lord make His face to shine upon you and be gracious to
    you

---

whether or not Jesus really meant that any part of the final judgment will rest on how one treated the Jews; but the point is fairly clear that the Almighty does care how His people get treated: "...he who touches you, touches the apple of His eye..." Zechariah 2:8.

The Lord lift up His countenance upon you and give you
    peace

It was my great privilege to deliver this brief talk to two
congregations while I was in Spain, and to pray for and bless the
nation at a number of other times and places.

Towards the end of the trip we visited the city of Cordoba. While
we were there, we got to take a walking tour of the Jewish
quarter, which has become something of a tourist trap. There is a
statue there of Moses Maimonides, a famous twelfth century
Rabbi, in a square near where he used to live and write.
Maimonides, also known to the Jews as Rambam, was the author
of one of the earliest compilations of Jewish law for the ordinary
man (as opposed to the Torah scholar). The synagogue that he
attended is still standing in Cordoba and is one of the tourist
attractions.

It was there in Cordoba that God reminded me that whatever else
I may be, I am a Jewish man, that He takes that seriously, and
that I should, too.

I wasn't sure exactly what He meant by that, but after that the
Holy Spirit started showing me things related to the Judaism of
Jesus' day. It took a few years for me to recognize that most of
these revelations fit neatly into an outline that followed the
Sermon on the Mount. Before that, the Sermon was a mystery to
me, as I said at the beginning. It's a bit clearer now, and it all
sounds very Jewish. So I wrote down the outline and proposed a
class to my leaders at the time, then taught the class in Adult
Sunday School.

At the end of this chapter you will see the current, adjusted
version of the outline that I used for the class, which I will be
following in this book. If you read the outline you will see that
the entire Sermon on the Mount can be expressed as a single,
English sentence:

"God wants you to model His character, so give Him your whole-hearted devotion and He will reproduce His character in you."

I have also included, as Appendix A, a harmony between the Sermon on the Mount in Matthew's gospel and the same teachings as they appear in Luke's gospel. Luke has what appears to be a version of the same sermon in his chapter 6,[17] but a lot of Matthew's content is missing from Luke 6. The missing content appears in other contexts and at different times in Luke's gospel, in chapters 11, 12, and 14. I find that Luke's version sometimes provides details that illuminate what Jesus meant, and at those times I'll be including it in my discussion.

## The Point of This Book

What I want to get across is this: when Matthew's gospel tells us that Jesus went up on a hill and began lecturing his disciples in Matthew 5:1, it was a Jewish Rabbi of the Second Temple Period[18] that was seating his religiously-aware, Jewish *talmidim* on a hillside in Galilee and explaining Judaism to them as he wanted them to practice it. Rabbi Jesus was restoring to Judaism the manner of serving the God of Israel that the Father had intended from the beginning.

He was doing it for us as much as He was doing it for them. And not just for us; for everybody. As we will see as we progress

---

[17] See Luke 6:17-48. Because of Luke 6:17, this is called the "Sermon on the Plain." It could have been the same occasion Matthew records, and it was a plateau on the mountainside. Or, Jesus may have delivered versions of the same sermon on different occasions and in different places. Or, the Sermon on the Mount in Matthew could possibly be an editor's gathering of several talks that Jesus did on different occasions into a single narrative. I'm treating the Sermon on the Mount as a single, cohesive sermon, and I'll leave it to scholars more austere than I (or more interested in the topic) to wrangle over whether that's really what it was.

[18] I explain "Second Temple Period" at the beginning of chapter three.

through the chapters, Jesus knew that He was beginning to establish the kingdom of heaven on earth, and He was laying out principles of conduct for life within it.

When God chose Israel as "His Chosen People," He was not choosing them only to save Israel and let the rest of the nations rot; He was choosing them with the intent of saving all the nations through them. When Israel failed to deliver, God said, "Ok, I'll do it myself,"[19] and sent "His own arm," His Messiah, the version of Israel that genuinely reflects His nature.[20]

When God chooses the Church in the Messiah, He is doing the same, as a fulfillment of the same plan. We are not chosen simply to fly off to heaven, and to hell with the rest; we are chosen to save those who have been lost.[21] As Paul said, the Gentiles are being "grafted in" to the existing olive tree, his metaphor for the Israelite nation, God's people.[22] God's work in the Messiah is the next step in His redemptive work through Israel. Jesus' instruction, as Jewish as it is, is for the Church, and not just for the Church but for all the nations; it applies to us now. He said so clearly, and so did His Apostles. I'll expand on this a little in the next chapter.

Now, we don't have to become Second Temple Jews in order to serve Jesus properly. That was the matter decided by the Jerusalem Council in Acts 15, the first Church council. Christian baptism has taken the place of circumcision as the required token

---

[19] I'm paraphrasing Isaiah 59:15b-16.

[20] Galatians 3:16

[21] I'm fairly sure that what Paul meant by "election" was not "there's a small number of us whom God predestined to be saved, and tough luck on the rest", but rather "We, the Church, are God's Chosen (just as the nation of Israel was God's Chosen) and our role is to save the rest." NT Wright talks of this in *What Saint Paul Really Said,* William B. Eerdmans Publishing Company, Grand Rapids, MI, 1997, p. 94. John, the Apostle, also talks of this in John 3:17. And Peter, the Apostle, also talks of it in I Peter 2:9-10.

[22] Romans 11:16-24

to enter the community of the redeemed.[23] The only parts of the Law that Gentiles have to obey as law are the parts that keep them from worshiping idols, and possibly the rest of the Noahide laws.[24] As Paul explained to Jews in Rome, when a believer—Jew or Gentile—walks in the Holy Spirit, that believer fulfills the righteousness that the Law required.[25]

In fact, far too many Protestants try to turn us into Second Temple Jews when they treat the New Testament the same way that some of the Pharisees of Jesus' day treated the Law of Moses, as rules that must be obeyed verbatim without understanding. That approach was a mistake in Judaism, and it's a mistake in Christianity, too.[26] What we have received is a relationship with a living, caring, active God, not a set of religious rules that we're obliged to keep by rote. Jesus did not rescue Gentiles from the Law just to place them under a newer, better, New Testament law.

Nor do we have to practice the festivals and rituals of the Torah, though doing so does no harm so long as we don't try to force those practices on others. We can be Jews or act like Jews, but we must not be Judaizers.[27]

---

[23] Colossians 2:11-12

[24] There are several theories regarding what was really the purpose of the decree in Acts 15:20 and 29. It may have been a short form of the Noahic covenant from Genesis 9, which I discuss briefly in chapter three (this is what I think); it may have been a summary of law from Leviticus 17-18; it may have been a concession to Jewish dietary laws; or it may have been something else entirely that we don't understand. Everybody agrees, though, that avoiding idolatry was at least part of the main point, so I used that shortened thought here. See https://www.gci.org/bible/acts/decree2 for a decent discussion.

[25] Romans 8:4

[26] That's actually part of the point of Matthew 5. I'll discuss this briefly in chapter six.

[27] Paul, the Apostle, spent a good deal of his ministry actively opposing those who insisted that Gentiles who embraced Christianity must enter the community of faith by being circumcised and then must proceed to obey the

Most American Jews really know very little of the Judaism I will be describing in this book. Few of us have studied *Talmud*; we're Jews more by descent than by practice. I spent most of my adulthood failing to recognize much of what Jesus and His disciples were doing; if I had studied *Talmud*, I would have recognized more of it. So please don't be surprised if you take some of the details I explain in this book to your Jewish friends and they've never heard of them before. That's sadly common.

It turns out, though, that understanding Jewish practices and teachings from Jesus' day sheds light on a lot of what Jesus had to say and makes it clearer how it may apply to us in our current lives. So, using Rabbi Jesus' Sermon on the Mount as a guide, I'm going to be introducing you to Jewish practices that may clarify His teaching. Follow me...

---

rest of Jewish Law. Theologians call these opponents of Paul "Judaizers." There are modern Judaizers as well. Some of them teach things that sound similar to what I'm writing here, explaining the Jewish context of the New Testament. It's good to consider that context, but don't let them force you to obey the Law. Paul was correct: Gentiles are not under that Law. I explain what that means in chapter three, along with a bunch of information about Judaism and history that you will need if you want to understand Jesus and Paul. Just turn a few pages and you're there...

## Outline of the Sermon on the Mount

### Subject: Life in the Kingdom of God

| | |
|---|---|
| I. God wants you to model His character... | Matthew 5 |
| A. Ordinary believers are holy | (5:3-12) |
| B. Your job is to demonstrate God's character | (5:13-16) |
| C. The scriptures are your guide | (5:17-20) |
| D. God's character is your standard | |
| 1. Hold relationships in highest esteem | (5:21-26) |
| 2. Keep your desires ordinate | (5:27-30) |
| 3. Speak truth at all times | (5:31-37) |
| 4. Do good to all, not evil | (5:38-48) |
| | |
| II. ...so give Him your whole-hearted devotion... | Matthew 6-7:2 |
| A. Serve God, not reputation | (6:1-18) |
| B. Serve God, not wealth | (6:19-24) |
| C. Serve God, not self | (6:25-7:2) |
| | |
| III. ...and He will produce His character in you. | Matthew 7:3-27 |
| A. Stay humble | (7:3-6) |
| B. Pray for God's help | (7:7-12) |
| C. Be diligent | (7:13-14) |
| D. Stick to the Master's training | (7:15-23) |
| E. He will make you unshakable | (7:24-27) |

## Chapter 2: The Sermon Is For the Church

I have discovered to my surprise that the first thing I need to do when discussing the Sermon on the Mount is to insist that it really is relevant to modern Christians.

The importance of that explanation got driven home for me gently but clearly in November of 2016. My wife and I had traveled to Oregon to be with her family, and the whole bunch of us visited a Christian camp in Oregon's coastal mountains for Thanksgiving. We got to stay in comfortable, rustic-looking but modern cabins and take our leisure while the staff took care of Thanksgiving dinner. While there, we had the opportunity to hear an elderly, itinerant minister teach on the ministry of Jesus.

He was a lovely, decent man who had been faithful in his ministry for more than three decades, so I will not tell you his name as I discuss what I thought of his introduction.

It went something like this:

> You know that separator page in your Bible between the end of the book of Malachi and the beginning of the gospel of Matthew, the one that separates the Old Testament from the New Testament? You really ought to tear that page out of your Bible carefully and re-insert it between the end of John's gospel and the beginning of the book of Acts. Everything that happened in the gospels happened under the authority of the Old Covenant, during which time people were saved by obeying the Law—a Law that nobody was able to keep.

I remembered thinking something similar when I was younger, and I reflected on the large number of Christian believers who would agree with this fellow. When I returned from that trip, I mentioned to a friend of mine, a mature, intelligent, believing woman, what this fellow had said and discovered that that's what she thought, too. Whenever I ask people about it, I always hear some of them agreeing. It's a mistake that's apparently everywhere.

It's tempting to quibble with everything I found wrong in that fine fellow's introduction. I could quibble with the notion that anybody was ever "saved" by obeying the Law; there are at least five entire chapters in the New Testament explaining that that was never the case.[1] Or, I could quibble with the common but truly bizarre notion that God gave the Israelites a law that they could not keep; He actually said exactly the opposite in Deuteronomy 30:11, assuring them that the Law was not too difficult for them to keep.[2]

But I don't need to address those things to show how the Sermon on the Mount is relevant to the Church, so that's all that I will say about them. All I need to do today is to point out what every Christian really ought to know in their bones: nothing that Jesus said is irrelevant, and none of it will pass away.[3]

When Jesus rose from the dead and commissioned His disciples for their ministries, His instructions to them made it clear that all His earlier teaching was still relevant to their mission:

> All authority in heaven and on earth has been given to me. Go therefore and make disciples of all nations, baptizing them in the name of the Father and of the Son and of the Holy Spirit, **teaching them to observe all that I have commanded you.** And behold, I am with you always, to the end of the age.[4]

---

[1] Romans 2, Romans 4, Galatians 3 and 4, and Hebrews 11.

[2] But then, they didn't keep it anyhow. God had Moses predict that as well, in Deuteronomy 31 and 32.

[3] Matthew 24:35, Mark 13:31, Luke 21:33. None of the Synoptic gospel writers omitted that one of Jesus' sayings. That's a clue. It's important.

[4] Matthew 28:18-20, emphasis mine.

The Great Commission, as this is called, was actually the declaration by the new CEO of earth and heaven explaining His new regime. "I am in charge now," said Jesus. "So here is the way I want things done: you are to make disciples of all the nations, not just the Jews, the same way that I made disciples of you. You will (1) baptize them into the name of the Trinity, and (2) teach them to do everything I taught you. Whenever and wherever you do this, I'll back you up."

It is the second step in making disciples that concerns us here. In the Great Commission, Jesus commanded that we should be teaching the nations "all that I have commanded you" when we disciple them. Did He teach them the Sermon on the Mount? Yes, or no? If the answer is "yes," then we are supposed to be teaching the nations to observe what's in the Sermon on the Mount. There is no wiggle room that I can see.

For those who think that Jesus was teaching solely within the old covenant and that He introduced something entirely different after His resurrection, this should be the first indication that there is something seriously wrong with that interpretation. I will explain how it's wrong in greater length in the next chapter.

The truth is that the Old and New Testaments overlap. Yes, God's commands for the nation of Israel were still in force while Jesus was ministering. Yes, a new regime was put into play after Jesus rose from the dead. But Jesus, while He ministered on earth, was the prototype for the new regime. We are His *talmidim* (disciples), which means that we are supposed to be becoming just like Him.[5] He established the kingdom of God on the earth while He was here, and everything He taught was relevant to it. We have been building His kingdom here on Earth ever since,

---

[5] See Romans 8:29 or II Corinthians 3:18, two from among many such declarations in the New Testament. But even without those passages, "become like the Rabbi" is what disciples are supposed to do, as I will explain in chapter nine.

following His instructions which He delivered to His Apostles while they were with Him.

So, no, do not move the separator page in your Bible. It's right where it belongs. And do not consider the Sermon on the Mount to be Old Testament instruction. It's not that. We are still supposed to be observing what He taught. For that matter, if you've not been paying attention to what Jesus said in the gospels, perhaps you should revisit them and pay closer attention.

## We're Still Saved by Grace

I have also discovered to my surprise that when I begin talking about what Jews like Jesus and Paul meant by "the Law" that I have to reassure a lot of Protestant Christians that I'm not trying to place them back under "the Law." That is not my intent, nor will it be my result. We're all still under grace. I'm going to be telling you, though, what terms like "the Law" have always meant and what "we're not under the Law"[6] means specifically, which may challenge your understanding. That's what chapter three is about.

It is certainly the case that God does not call only good, decent people into His kingdom. In fact, He calls most of us while we're still pretty horribly wicked. That is very gracious of Him. But it is certainly not the case that God places no standard of conduct on His people. It has always been His intent to make people behave decently toward one another.

Christian teachers say "You don't have to do anything, He's done it all!" If by that they mean that God invites us into His kingdom on the basis of His sacrifice for us and not on the basis of our good conduct, and that furthermore He supplies by way of the Holy Spirit all the means by which we can change our ways so that we become like Him, then yes, they're right, and profoundly

---

[6] Romans 6:14

so. But if they mean that God has no interest in how we conduct ourselves in His name and that once we've prayed to be let in He doesn't expect anything else, they could not possibly be more wrong. As the Sermon on the Mount explains, the community of the kingdom of God is a community of love and devotion in which we are to be changed so that we accurately reflect the character of God, the Father. That is not contrary to grace; that is what God's grace produces.

## The Old Testament is Still Authoritative

Another thing: a disturbing number of Christians that I encounter think that "the Law" means "the Old Testament," and that "we're not under Law, we're under grace" means "We don't need the Old Testament anymore; we only need the New Testament." I've even heard people say that whoever quotes the Old Testament is by that simple act attempting to put believers under Law.

I understand that that's what a disturbing number of teachers have said, but I honestly can't imagine why they ever said it.

In the first place, the Jews never referred to any part of their scriptures as "the Law" besides the first five books, which they call the Torah. I will explain that in more detail in the next chapter.

In the second place, the Apostles all continued to use *Tanakh* (the Old Testament) even after Jesus rose from the dead. In his fairly slim set of letters in the New Testament, the Apostle Paul quoted *Tanakh* more than a hundred times, always as though it was authoritative for him and his audience. The scriptures that those oh-so-noble Bereans examined so carefully in Acts 17 were Old Testament scriptures, and they were examining them because Paul was teaching from them.[7] The "sacred writings" that Paul

---

[7] Acts 17:11. The pattern of Paul's proclamation in that region is described in Acts 17:2-3, in his visit to Thessalonika.

insisted were breathed out by God and were able to make
Timothy wise to the salvation of his soul were Old Testament
scriptures.[8] The scriptures that Paul told the Corinthians "…were
written down for our instruction, on whom the end of the ages
has come"[9] were not just Old Testament scriptures, they were
from the oldest of the Old Testament scriptures, the Torah.
Clearly, Paul thought that the Old Testament scriptures were still
relevant, as did all the other Apostles and as did the Lord Jesus.

The good news, of course, is that we have lots of examples in the
New Testament showing us how Old Testament scriptures ought
to be used by the Church. We've had that all along. If you're one
of those to whom the idea of using the Old Testament is
disturbing, all you need to do is pay attention as you read the
New Testament to how Jesus and the Apostles used Old
Testament scriptures when they used them, and follow their
example. It's truly not that difficult (though it is at times a bit
different from how we do it in the twenty-first century), and it
should not disturb any of your key beliefs.

That said, you should also be aware that in this book I am going
to be introducing you to places in the New Testament that are
built entirely on Old Testament lessons even though they don't
always quote the Old Testament directly.

Truly, if you're Christian there's no getting away from the Old
Testament. Christianity, properly understood, rests on the
foundation of *Tanakh*.

As Paul, the Apostle to the Gentiles, warned the Gentiles among
the Roman believers, speaking of Judaism as though it were an
olive tree:

> But if some of the branches were broken off, and you,
> although a wild olive shoot, were grafted in among the others

---

[8] II Timothy 3:14-17

[9] I Corinthians 10:11b

and now share in the nourishing root of the olive tree, do not be arrogant toward the branches. If you are, remember it is not you who support the root, but the root that supports you.[10]

Jesus is the Jewish Messiah. Everything that He taught rested on the truth of the Jewish scriptures. If you, as a Christian believer, do not understand Jesus' Judaism, then you will never completely understand what the Jewish Messiah and His Jewish Apostles were trying to get across to you. You can be "saved" without learning about Judaism, you can get to know God intimately, and you can understand lots of things; but you'll misunderstand a lot of what Jesus and His Apostles said. You can't interpret any passage in scripture properly without understanding its context—and Jesus' Judaism is the bedrock of the context.

---

[10] Romans 11:17-18

# Chapter 3: What Will Never Pass Away?

## Outline of the Sermon on the Mount
### Subject: Life in the Kingdom of God

| | |
|---|---|
| I. God wants you to model His character... | Matthew 5 |
| A. Ordinary believers are holy | (5:3-12) |
| B. Your job is to demonstrate God's character | (5:13-16) |
| **C. The scriptures are your guide** | **(5:17-20)** |
| D. God's character is your standard | |
| 1. Hold relationships in highest esteem | (5:21-26) |
| 2. Keep your desires ordinate | (5:27-30) |
| 3. Speak truth at all times | (5:31-37) |
| 4. Do good to all, not evil | (5:38-48) |
| | |
| II. ...so give Him your whole-hearted devotion... | Matthew 6-7:2 |
| A. Serve God, not reputation | (6:1-18) |
| B. Serve God, not wealth | (6:19-24) |
| C. Serve God, not self | (6:25-7:2) |
| | |
| III. ...and He will produce His character in you. | Matthew 7:3-27 |
| A. Stay humble | (7:3-6) |
| B. Pray for God's help | (7:7-12) |
| C. Be diligent | (7:13-14) |
| D. Stick to the Master's training | (7:15-23) |
| E. He will make you unshakable | (7:24-27) |

Before we rewind to the Beatitudes that Jesus used to introduce His sermon, let me explain the paragraph that is probably the most confusing claim in the Sermon on the Mount, a claim that convinces readers that Jesus intended to maintain the Jewish Law. That is not what He was saying, but to modern ears it sure sounds like it was.

Do not think that I have come to abolish the Law or the
Prophets; I have not come to abolish them but to fulfill them.
For truly, I say to you, until heaven and earth pass away, not
an iota, not a dot, will pass from the Law until all is
accomplished. Therefore whoever relaxes one of the least of
these commandments and teaches others to do the same will
be called least in the kingdom of heaven, but whoever does
them and teaches them will be called great in the kingdom of
heaven. For I tell you, unless your righteousness exceeds that
of the scribes and Pharisees, you will never enter the kingdom
of heaven.[1]

The editor-supplied heading over this paragraph in the English
Standard Version actually says, "Christ Came to Fulfill the Law,"
and I have heard any number of Christians express that they think
that's what Jesus intended. And that's not all. In my years of
interacting with Christians of all stripes, I've heard some declare,
based on this passage, that Jesus' theology was vastly different
from Paul's, others that Jesus meant that He was going to fulfill
prophecies, still others that the Sermon on the Mount was clearly
an Old Testament teaching that has no relevance to the New
Testament Church, and still others that Jesus was making
reference to His crucifixion.

None of those is entirely correct and a couple of them are
completely wrong. Jesus was actually endorsing the Jewish canon
of scripture, what Christians call the Old Testament and what
Jews call *Tanakh*. He was saying that the scriptures would not be
broken, a declaration which He made several times during His
ministry[2] and which is entirely consistent with Paul's apostolic
writing.

To understand why Jesus' words would have been taken that way
by His Jewish *talmidim*, we are going to have to review a bit of

---

[1] Matthew 5:17-20
[2] See John 10:35, Luke 24:27, Luke 24:44.

Jewish history and understand some common first century phrases.

## The Second Temple Period

The first temple was the one built by Solomon somewhere around 950 BCE near the start of the Davidic Monarchy, described in the Old Testament beginning in I Kings 5. The era of the monarchy under the House of David is called the First Temple Period. Modern Jews and historians consider the beginning of this period to be the golden age of the nation of Israel, when the nation covered a larger area than it has ever covered since and achieved its greatest wealth and influence.

Solomon's temple was destroyed around 587 BCE by the Babylonians under the leadership of Nebuchadnezzar II, and they took most of the Jews captive into Babylon. That was the end of the First Temple Period, and the beginning of the period called The Captivity.

Around 538 BCE, Jews began returning from what had in the meantime become the Persian Empire[3] and built the second temple under the leadership of Ezra the Priest. This is recorded in the Old Testament in the books of Ezra and Nehemiah. That was the beginning of the Second Temple Period. The Second Temple Period lasted until 70 CE when the Romans disassembled the temple brick by brick during the First Jewish-Roman War, about forty years after Jesus was crucified and rose from the dead.

Christian students of the Bible tend to think of the Second Temple Period as four hundred years of blank space between the end of Malachi, chronologically the last of the Old Testament prophetic books, and John the Baptist, who introduced the

---

[3] See II Chronicles 36:20, which is consistent with what we know of the Persian Empire from archaeology.

ministry of Jesus in the gospel accounts. If they are studying only the Old and New Testaments, that's how it looks.

In actual fact, though, the Second Temple Period was a busy time for Jewish writers. All the stories and proverbs included in what Protestants call the Apocrypha were written during that period: titles include *Tobit*, *Judit*, *Maccabees*, *The Wisdom of Solomon*, and a number of others. There were also more than a dozen apocalyptic works produced by Jewish authors with titles like *The Book of Jubilees*, *The Book of Enoch*, *The Apocalypse of Zephaniah*, *The Apocalypse of Abraham*, and so on. A Jewish philosopher named Philo produced a number of apologetic works that are still available to modern scholars. Jewish scholars produced a major Greek translation of the Old Testament for the Ptolemys, who ruled Egypt, called the Septuagint. And, as I will explain in more detail in a moment, a lot of legal analysis of the Torah took place and became part of the Jewish culture during that period.

## Occupied and Free Judea

After Ezra built the second temple, Jews in Judea continued to live under Persian rule for about two hundred years. Then, in 332 BCE, Alexander the Great moved through the area of Judea and conquered it, on his way to conquering the rest of the known world. From then until Alexander's death about ten years later, the Jews lived under Macedonian rule.

Alexander did not make arrangements for his succession, so when he died in 323 BCE his kingdom fell apart. Judea fell under the rule of one of Alexander's generals named Ptolemy, who declared himself Pharaoh in Egypt. The Ptolemys ruled Judea as part of Egypt for a little more than a hundred years.

The Ptolemys fought a series of wars against another group of Alexander's former generals who had settled in Syria called the

Seleucids. Around 200 BCE the Seleucids took over control of Judea as a result of one of those wars.

While the Seleucids ruled Judea, Antiochus IV of the Seleucid empire decided that he was going to Hellenize the Jews (that is, he wanted them to become Greeks.) He outlawed circumcision, placed statues of Greek gods in the Jewish temple, and ordered the Jews to make sacrifices of unclean animals to the Greek gods, among other oppressive policies intended to stamp out Judaism.

The apocryphal book entitled *I Maccabees* tells how that went. It tells of a man named Mattathias who lived under the tyranny of Antiochus IV in a small town called Modin in the mountains of Judea. When Mattathias saw a fellow Jew performing a sacrifice of an unclean animal in obedience to the Seleucids, he became angry and killed the man. Then he fled into the hills with his five sons and started a rebellion. Mattathias' son Judah the Maccabee became the primary leader of the rebellion ("Maccabee" means "hammer of God"). By what everybody considered a major miracle of God, the Maccabean revolt succeeded in driving the Seleucids, with their far larger and more modern army, out of Judea entirely. This took place around 160 BCE. The modern Jewish celebration of Hanukah celebrates their victory over the Seleucids and the miracle that took place then.

The Maccabees established an independent Jewish nation in Judea under a dynasty called the Hasmonean dynasty. The Hasmoneans ruled independently for around a hundred years but gave way when the Roman general Pompeii invaded in 63 BCE. The Romans permitted the Hasmoneans to continue ruling under their dominion. Herod the Great, who was ruling Judea when Jesus was born, married into the family of the Hasmonean kings; his wife Mariamne I was a Hasmonean of the sixth generation from Mattathias. Herod was not a Jew, though; he was an Idumean, which was the Roman name for the group called the Edomites in the Old Testament.

Thereafter, Herod and his family continued to rule under the Romans until the Jewish wars of independence began in 66 CE (Jesus lived, ministered, and died during this period). Beginning in 66 CE, the Jews fought three, separate wars of independence against the Romans, and they lost all three. After the first war, called the Great Revolt or the First Roman-Jewish War, the second temple was torn down completely. After the third war, the Bar Kokhba Rebellion in 135 CE, the Jews were banned from living in Jerusalem, the Emperor Hadrian removed the name "Judea" from Roman maps and replaced it with "Syria Palaestina,"[4] and the Jewish population of Judea was mostly either killed or sold into slavery.

## The Rise of Rabbinic Judaism

The name "Jews" to describe the Hebrews came from the name of the main tribe that was represented in the southern kingdom of Israel, "Judah." When Israel split from the House of David in response to Rehoboam's tyranny,[5] the southern kingdom consisted of

- the tribe of Judah,

- the remnant of the tribe of Benjamin after it nearly had been wiped out at the battle of Gibeah,[6]

- the majority of the Levites, who had lived among the cities of Israel but had fled to Judah after Jeroboam removed their authority,[7]

- whatever Hebrews from other tribes who happened to live in the cities of Judah,[8] and

---

[4] "Palaestina," from which we get the modern "Palestine," was a Latin reference to the Philistines. Hadrian wanted to erase any memory of Jews having lived in the region.

[5] I Kings 12, II Chronicles 10

[6] Judges 19-21

[7] II Chronicles 11:13-15

- those Hebrews from the other tribes who refused to worship the calves that Jeroboam created for them in Bethel and Dan.[9]

This took place during the 10th century BCE, a bit more than three hundred years before Jerusalem was captured by the Babylonians.

The Hebrew religion under the Davidic kings was a temple-centered religion. The only place where sacrifices were proper was the temple in Jerusalem.[10] There were, however, plenty of reports in *Tanakh* of Hebrews practicing sacrifices in "the high places," which were probably sacred spots from pagan times.[11] This practice was apparently one of the reasons for which God eventually removed the Hebrews from their homeland.[12]

After the first temple was destroyed, the Jews in captivity in Babylon had to develop a form of their religion that did not rely on the temple. The Judaism they developed focused on the Torah, the five books of the Law delivered by Moses. They created meeting houses called synagogues[13] in which the Torah was read publicly and in which students gathered to study Torah. They developed a series of traditions and patterns surrounding the commands in the Torah to codify how the Laws of Moses were to be practiced. They also began maintaining commentaries by leading scholars called "Rabbis" regarding the proper

---

[8] I Kings 12:17, II Chronicles 10:17

[9] II Chronicles 11:16-17

[10] Leviticus 17:1-8, Deuteronomy 12:1-14

[11] You can follow a history of Israelite worship at the high places by reading I Kings 3:2-3, I Kings 12:31-32, I Kings 15:14, I Kings 22:43, II Kings 12:3, II Kings 14:4, and II Kings 23:19-20, but it's mentioned in quite a few other places.

[12] See, for example, Jeremiah 2:19-20, Jeremiah 3:1b-2, Jeremiah 17:1-3.

[13] It's from a Greek word, "*sunagoga*", meaning a gathering. Nobody seems to know what Hebrew word they used to describe their gatherings while in captivity.

interpretation of the Torah. One of the major differences between temple worship and synagogue worship was that while only priests of the family of Aaron could perform the offices of the temple, any Jew who was *bar mitzvah* ("son of the commandment") was permitted to read the Torah or other scriptures in the synagogue.[14]

When Ezra led some of the Jews back to Judea from Babylon and built the second temple, a number of Jews remained in Babylon, and from there some eventually traveled to other major cities around the known world. The sacrifices spelled out in Torah were carried out in the new temple in Jerusalem as before, but synagogue worship and the study of Torah continued in all the places outside of Jerusalem, and part of the temple in Jerusalem was used to study Torah as well.

After the Maccabees successfully created an independent Jewish state around 160 BCE, there was a new influx of Jews from Babylon and elsewhere in the world into the area that we now call Israel. A number of them established towns and centers of learning in the region called Galilee around the lake Kinneret, which modern readers know as the Sea of Galilee. The region of Galilee became a center of Rabbinic Judaism. The ruins of the synagogue in Capernaum, on the north shore of Kinneret, are the largest synagogue found by archaeologists that was built before the fifteenth century CE.[15] In the *Mishna*, which I'll talk about in a moment, quotes from Rabbis who lived in Capernaum outnumber quotes from Rabbis of all other places combined.[16]

---

[14] *Bar mitzvah* is a ceremony that most Gentiles recognize. It celebrates a Jewish male reaching the age of majority (thirteen years old) by allowing him to read from the Torah scrolls. Modern Judaism includes females as well.

[15] The large Capernaum synagogue dates from the fourth century CE. There's an older synagogue beneath it, probably from the first century.

[16] I learned much of this from the lectures of a teacher from Focus on the Family named Ray Vander Laan. Vander Laan is an ordained Rabbi and also a graduate of Westminster Theological Seminary. He does a long talk about Judaism of Jesus' day called "Follow the Rabbi". I found audio of the entire Follow the Rabbi lecture, about ten hours long in all, at

The Rabbis of Galilee were reputed to be particularly strict in their observance of Torah.[17]

After the second temple was destroyed and the residents of Jerusalem were scattered by the Romans in 70 CE, the center of Jewish culture shifted from Jerusalem to Galilee, and Rabbinic Judaism became the only form of Judaism that was viable. Pretty much all of modern Judaism descends from the Rabbis of Galilee that lived before and shortly after Jesus.

## *Halakha* (The Law)

The primary focus of Rabbinic Judaism was "the Law." "The Law" was also the subject of a great deal of the Apostle Paul's writing and a lot of Jesus' teaching. For that reason Christians need to know what is meant by the phrase "the Law," but in my experience they usually don't.

The key point for modern Christians is that the Old Testament is not "the Law," and "the Law" is not the Old Testament. "The Law" is either a direct reference to the five books of Moses, or a broader reference to what Jews call *halakha*, their entire system of law, which begins with the five books of Moses but is mostly outside the Bible.

When a Jew uses the phrase "the Law," his most direct meaning is the first five books of *Tanakh*. The Greek/Latin names of those books are Genesis, Exodus, Leviticus, Numbers, and Deuteronomy. Jews call these five books *B'raysheet*, *Shemot*, *Vayikrah*, *Bamidbar*, and *D'varim*, and we call the collection of

---

http://oneinjesus.info/2008/10/ray-vander-laans-follow-the-rabbi-lectures/. I found a shorter version of the same lecture, only four hours long, on YouTube at https://www.youtube.com/watch?v=tE5xyKdIeXM. A lot of what I say about rabbinic practice in this book was influenced by Vander Laan, though I got some of it from my upbringing and other general reading as well.

[17] Turnage, Mark, "First-Century Galilee: Contextualizing Jesus," http://enrichmentjournal.ag.org/201402/201402_024_Galilee.cfm.

these five books Torah (modern scholars sometimes refer to it as the Pentateuch). Jewish tradition holds that Moses wrote the entire Torah (except for the last eight verses, which describe his death), so the Torah is also referred to as "the five books of Moses," "the Law of Moses," or sometimes simply "Moses," and it's also referred to at times as "the Law." Jews of the Second Temple Period used the same terms, as we can see when we read the New Testament.

However, when Jews use the phrase "the Law," we often mean it in a wider sense. These references include what we call the Oral Law. As we will see, Jews of the Second Temple Period sometimes meant it that way, too.

Jewish scholars had located and codified six hundred thirteen commands out of the five books of the Law,[18] but the Law did not spell out what all those commands meant that they were supposed to do. For example, the Law forbade them to carry burdens on the Sabbath. However, it did not contain any definition of what constitutes carrying a burden. If a man takes off his jacket and drapes it over his arm on a hot Sabbath day, is he violating the Sabbath by carrying a burden? What if he hands a loaf of bread to a beggar at his door on the Sabbath? Forbidden burden, or not?

We might dismiss such concerns as trivial from our twenty-first-century vantage point, but consider: the nation of Israel had suffered a calamity many times worse than what America suffered in the World Trade Center attack in 2001, and they had suffered that catastrophe explicitly because they had not obeyed the Law delivered by Moses. The question of how they were to

---

[18] The count varied according to which Rabbi was cataloguing them, but all the counts were close to that number. Six hundred thirteen is the count produced by Moses Maimonides, the famous twelfth century Spanish Rabbi whose work heavily influenced modern Judaism, so that's the count that most modern Jews accept. I talked about visiting his statue in Cordoba back in the first chapter, remember?

obey that Law in the aftermath of that national calamity was central to their entire way of life, and they regarded it as the key to their personal and national standing before God.

Jewish scholars therefore generated a complete set of rules and definitions to explain how to go about obeying the six hundred thirteen commands in the Torah. They thought of this as "building a fence around the Torah," meaning that if one kept these rules they would never violate the commands of the Torah even by accident.[19] They said that the Oral Law explaining these things was given to Moses on Sinai at the same time that he received the stone tablets containing the Ten Commandments. Whether it is true that God gave the Oral Law to Moses at that time or not, it is clear that a fairly complete set of rules was already in place by the time that Jesus began His ministry. We know this because the New Testament contains several references to those rules which I'll point to in a moment and throughout this book.

Not all Jews were equally involved with this rule-making. There were divisions in Judaism during the Second Temple period.[20] While the Rabbinic system was developing, Jewish leaders responsible for the temple in Jerusalem held to an older form in which the traditions of the Oral Law were mostly ignored. These Jews appear in the New Testament as "chief priests" or "Sadducees," and their beliefs tended to dismiss miracles and references to *olam ha-bah*, "the world to come."

By contrast, the Pharisees mentioned in the New Testament were strong believers in the Oral Law. While it is not exactly clear

---

[19] *Talmud*, Tractate *Avot* 1.1. The *Gemara* following that passage in the *Talmud* discusses what they meant by "fence." https://www.jewishvirtuallibrary.org/tractate-avot-chapter-1. I also explain this further in chapter seven.

[20] A good discussion of the divisions in Judaism during the Second Temple Period can be found at http://www.myjli.com/debates/index.php/lesson-1/challenge-and-transformation-second-temple-and-rabbinic-judaism/.

what the connection was between Rabbinic Judaism and the Pharisees, it appears that the Pharisees represented the most serious developers of the Oral Law from the days of the Maccabees until the destruction of the second temple.[21] Pharisees referred to Jews who were unschooled in their legal system as *am ha-aretz*, "people of the land," and considered them to be second-class Jews.[22]

The scribes would have been professional creators and copyists of written records, and some of these were likely employed by the Jewish leaders of the temple to copy and maintain sacred writings. Where the New Testament mentions "scribes," though, it seems often to connect them with the Pharisees and their version of the Law, so it seems likely that some of them were employed writing down the opinions of the Rabbis as they were being spoken, even while those opinions were still considered "Oral Law."

For a long time Jewish leaders responsible for teaching the Oral Law resisted writing it down. Keeping it oral encouraged closer relations between students and teachers, and that seemed to them to be a better way to maintain traditions.[23] However, after the Jews' three disastrous wars of independence against the Romans in the first and second centuries CE, so many Rabbis had been killed that some of those who were left were afraid that the Oral Law would be forgotten.

Reacting to this, around 200 CE a leading Rabbi named Yehudah HaNasi ("Judah the Prince") decided to write down all the traditions of the Oral Law. He composed sixty three treatises or "tractates" in six major sections organized by legal topic. This set

---

[21] There is a good discussion of the Pharisees in Skarsaune, Oskar, *In the Shadow of the Temple: Jewish Influences on Early Christianity*, Downer's Grove, IL, Intervarsity Press, 2002, pp. 117-122.

[22] John 7:48-49 represents this point of view, I think, though some scholars might dispute this.

[23] http://www.jewishvirtuallibrary.org/the-oral-law-talmud-and-mishna

of sixty three tractates, the Jews call *Mishna*, a Hebrew word meaning "to study by repetition." Rabbi Yehudah and later writers also added commentary and discussions by Rabbis about the *Mishna* showing some different ways that the Law had been interpreted. These commentaries by the Rabbis, Jews call *Gemara*, a Hebrew word meaning "completion." The two collections, *Mishna* and *Gemara*, collated together into a single volume are called *Talmud*, from a Hebrew word meaning "to learn." The Babylonian *Talmud* was completed around the fifth century CE.

Today there are actually two *Talmuds*, the Jerusalem or Palestinian *Talmud* and the Babylonian *Talmud*. They both present the same set of laws, but they contain different rabbinic commentaries about those laws (same *Mishna*, different *Gemara*). The Jerusalem *Talmud* is a little bit older but its commentary covers only part of the *Mishna*; the Babylonian is more complete. These days if you see a quote from the *Talmud* and it does not specify which one, it's probably from the Babylonian *Talmud*. (I follow that convention in this book.)

This body of law that the Rabbis produced to govern Jewish conduct, including Torah, *Talmud*, and additional commentary and stories called *midrashim*, Jews call *halakha*. Learn that word, because that's what Jews mean when we use the phrase "the Law" in the broader sense. *Halakha* is the whole, complex body of Jewish Law and the system that maintains and interprets that Law.

Even though the *Talmud* was not formally written until 200 CE and not completed for another three hundred years after that, the Oral Law was being used by Rabbinic Jews long before then. In Paul's and Jesus' day, when they talked about the Law they were sometimes referring in the narrowest sense to the five books of Moses, but at other times were referring in a broader sense to the entire *halakha* as it stood in their day, both written text and oral tradition. They took it for granted that the listener would know from the context in what sense they meant "Law."

It is crucial to notice that in Jewish usage "the Law" never included most of what Christians call the Old Testament. The primary reference was only to the five books of Moses. The secondary, broader reference was to what became the *Talmud* and related discussion, the Oral Law. "Law" did not and does not include the books of the Prophets, the Psalms, the Proverbs, the books of the Kings and the Chronicles, the stories of Ruth, Job, or Esther, or any of the other Old Testament books.[24]

So when Paul explained that Christians "are not under Law but under grace,"[25] he was not saying that *Tanakh*, the Old Testament, was irrelevant or that it had been superseded. On the contrary, he said several times that the Old Testament scriptures were still applicable. I discussed this back in chapter two. The Old Testament has never stopped being relevant.

Let me say this again: "the Law" is not the Old Testament, and the Old Testament is not "the Law." To think of "the Law" as the Old Testament is not a possible interpretation or a plausible point of view; it's simply a mistake made by people who do not understand Judaism.

In the New Testament, the most explicit reference to the rules that became the *Talmud* occurs in Mark's gospel, in chapter 7:

---

[24] As so often happens when we attempt to systematize the New Testament, the scriptures actually throw a small wrench into my neat formulation. There is one spot where Jesus referred to Psalm 82:1 as "your Law" to the Pharisees, in John 10:34. I suspect that Jesus was simply using the word "law" to make the Pharisees uncomfortable, and my support for that is Jesus calling it "your Law" and not "our Law" or "the Law." He may have been making a derisive reference to their habit of worshiping the scriptures, making laws out of things that were not law. But it does puzzle me a little.

[25] Romans 6:14

Now when the Pharisees gathered to him, with some of the scribes who had come from Jerusalem, they saw that some of his disciples ate with hands that were defiled, that is, unwashed. (For the Pharisees and all the Jews do not eat unless they wash their hands properly, holding to the tradition of the elders, and when they come from the marketplace, they do not eat unless they wash. And there are many other traditions that they observe, such as the washing of cups and pots and copper vessels and dining couches.) And the Pharisees and the scribes asked him, "Why do your disciples not walk according to the tradition of the elders, but eat with defiled hands?" And he said to them, "Well did Isaiah prophesy of you hypocrites, as it is written,

> "'This people honors me with their lips,
> but their heart is far from me;
> in vain do they worship me,
> teaching as doctrines the commandments of men.'"[26]

What Mark was describing can now be found in Tractate *Yadayim* in the *Talmud*. However, since *Talmud* was not formally written down in Jesus' day, we do not know for certain whether the laws then were exactly as written later by Yehudah HaNasi.

There are other references to *Talmud* in the New Testament. For example, John 7:22-23 discusses rules under which circumcision may be performed on the Sabbath, rules that show up in Tractate *Shabbat* 19. In John 7:37-39 when Jesus declared "whoever is thirsty, let him come to me and drink," He was attending the water-drawing festival mentioned in Tractate *Sukkah* 51a and 51b and declaring Himself to be the very thing that the festival was celebrating; I'll explain this as part of an illustration in chapter seven. Matthew 19:3-9 discusses a dispute from Tractate *Gittin* 90 that I will address in chapter six.

---

[26] Mark 7:1-7.

Mark's reference to the Oral Law also described Jesus' attitude toward it: He called it "the commandments of men" indicating that God was not the author of those rules. He said that attempting to serve God by obeying those rules was useless.

Jesus actually said a great deal about the Jewish religious legal system in the New Testament. A lot of what He said was negative, but in general we should think of Jesus, not as rejecting the Law, but as a fellow-Jew critiquing His contemporaries' handling of it. As we will see in chapter six, a large portion of Matthew 5 discusses possible shortcomings in interpretation of the law of God but does so from the point of view of an authoritative Rabbi adjusting *halakha*, upholding the notion that God's law is good. Matthew 23 does the same. A number of Jesus' parables were rewrites of common stories used by the Rabbis to illustrate important points of *halakha*, though sometimes Jesus modified them to teach different lessons.

*Halakha* is God's law for the Jews, encompassing both the Law of Moses and the Oral Law. Typical Jewish teaching regarding Gentiles said that they were subject only to the laws spoken by God after Noah's flood in Genesis 9, called the Noahide Laws by modern scholars. Because Noah was the ancestor of both Jews and Gentiles, the covenant God made with him was held to apply to everybody. The Rabbis culled seven laws from the passage, forbidding blasphemy, idolatry, adultery, murder, robbery, and eating the flesh of a living animal, plus a requirement for civil law and law courts.[27] Gentiles who kept those laws were considered "righteous pagans" by the Rabbis, and many of them taught that such righteous pagans had a place in *olam ha-bah*, "the world to come." Notice that the Ten Commandments never actually applied to the Gentiles; the Ten were Jewish law.

Paul, the Apostle, declared that Christians were no longer subject to the Law of Moses.[28] What he meant was that Christians are not

---

[27] *Talmud*, Tractate *Sanhedrin* 56a.

[28] See, for example, Romans 6:14 and Galatians 5:18.

subject to *halakha*: the six hundred thirteen commands in the Torah, plus the Oral Law as it stood in his day. That was the Law that Paul studied before he was converted on the road to Damascus. He claims to have studied under Gamaliel, a Rabbi mentioned in the *Talmud* as one of the greatest teachers in the annals of Judaism, so we know that it was early Talmudic Judaism that Paul studied.[29]

Paul understood that Gentiles had never been subject to *halakha*. That was among the reasons that he objected so strenuously to Gentiles like the believers in Galatia allowing themselves to be subjected to circumcision in order that they could become members of the community of God.[30] Paul taught consistently that they were not required to obey the Jewish law, but instead became members of the household of faith by declaring their devotion to Christ Jesus through baptism.

Scholars argue over whether Paul thought that *halakha* still applied to Jewish Christians. My interpretation is that apparently he taught that Jewish believers were not required to keep *halakha* but that he himself continued to practice *halakha* throughout his life. As I said in my first chapter, nothing is harmed by Jewish believers in Jesus keeping *halakha* so long as they don't insist on controlling the behavior of others with their practices.

The Law to which Christian believers are not subject is *halakha*, the Jewish legal system. We do not have to keep all six hundred thirteen laws in the Torah, nor do we have to follow the instructions in the *Mishna* explaining how to obey those laws. If

---

[29] See Acts 22:3. There are actually six Gamaliels mentioned at length in the *Talmud*, all from the same family in successive generations, and three others mentioned only in passing. The Gamaliel who was alive about the time Jesus died, known as Gamaliel the Elder, was the first. He was said to be the grandson of the great Rabbi Hillel. He's also likely the same Gamaliel who advised the Sanhedrin to leave the disciples alone in Acts 5:34-40, and the same who trained Paul. See https://www.myjewishlearning.com/article/rabban-gamaliel/.

[30] See Galatians 1:6-9, Galatians 3:1-6, Galatians 6:12-16.

we were to review Romans 8 at this point, we would be reminded that we do not need to obey those laws because when we obey God in the Spirit we practice the righteousness that those laws were intended to create.[31] Nearly all of Paul's letters contain descriptions of what that conduct is supposed to look like.

Since most of my readers will never have come across anything from the *Talmud* except possibly a few isolated quotes, I have included a small section from the Babylonian *Talmud* as Appendix B at the end of the book so you can get a feel for what sorts of discussions one can find there. The section I chose was a detailed discussion of who might be violating the Sabbath law against carrying burdens on the occasion that a beggar came to a person's door on the Sabbath and either gave that person something or received something from him. After reading a few pages of this intricate, pains-taking discussion you can understand pretty clearly why the crowds listening to Jesus reacted as the writer of Matthew's gospel described at the end of the Sermon on the Mount:

> And when Jesus finished these sayings, the crowds were astonished at his teaching, for he was teaching them as one who had authority, and not as their scribes.[32]

Later on I will mention other things implied by that observation, but for now, just comparing to the *Mishna* will show you why Rabbi Jesus' teaching might have seemed like a breath of fresh air to those studying Torah under the Rabbis of Jesus' day. They might have agreed with Him: "Hey, his yoke is easy, and his burden is light."[33]

---

[31] See in particular Romans 8:4, and in general Romans 8:1-13; see also Galatians 5:13-26.

[32] Matthew 7:28-29

[33] Matthew 11:30. "Yoke" is a term used by Torah scholars to describe a particular Rabbi's body of teaching.

## The Law and the Prophets

In several places in the New Testament the writers or speakers refer to "the Law and the Prophets," or sometimes to "Moses and the Prophets," or even "the Law of Moses and the Prophets." "The Law" in all those places refers to the five books of Moses explicitly. However, to understand what they meant by the entire phrase, "the Law and the Prophets," I will have to explain how we Jews organize our Bible.

If Gentile Christians of the 21st century were to pick up a Bible printed by the Jewish Publication Society or some other Jewish publisher and look in the table of contents, they might be confused for a little while because the books will not appear in the order they expect. It starts out looking the same, but then Isaiah shows up where they would have expected the Psalms to be, the Psalms and Proverbs are towards the back, and the last book in the volume is Chronicles. If they took the time to examine it carefully they would discover that all the books in the Protestant Old Testament are there in the Jewish canon as well but in a different order.[34]

The Jewish canon contains three sections:

1) *Torah* ("Instruction"): also called "the Law," these are the five books of Moses, the Hebrew names of which are *B'raysheet, Shemot, Vayikrah, Bamidbar,* and *D'varim.* We know them by their Greek/Latin names: Genesis, Exodus, Leviticus, Numbers, Deuteronomy;

2) *Nevi'im* ("Prophets"): the works of the three major and twelve minor prophets plus those narrative works that Jewish tradition says were prophetic: Joshua, Judges, Samuel, and Kings;

---

[34] All the books in the Jewish and Protestant canons are also present in the Catholic and Orthodox canons, but the Catholic and Orthodox canons both contain a few books that do not appear in the Jewish or Protestant canons.

3) *Ketuvim* ("Writings"): other narrative works, plus songs
   and poems.

For Protestants familiar with the Old Testament, it is interesting
to see that while Samuel and Kings are in the Prophets (*Nevi'im*),
Chronicles is not; it's at the end of the Writings *(Ketuvim)*. That's
because in Jewish tradition, Jeremiah allegedly wrote the books
of Samuel and Kings as prophetic declaration to Israel, but Ezra
most likely wrote the Chronicles to remind the Jews of their
heritage after the captivity. Jeremiah was a prophet, Ezra was not.
In the same way, Daniel does not appear in the Prophets
*(Nevi'im)* because Daniel, though he was a great man, was not a
prophet.[35] Lamentations appears in the Writings (*Ketuvim*) as
well, though nobody I've asked has been able to explain why.

I'm speaking of Samuel, Kings, and Chronicles each as one book
because each of them were originally single books and were
divided later by Christian scholars. Ezra and Nehemiah were also
written originally as a single book, and were divided into separate
books later.

I have referred a few times to the Jewish version of the Old
Testament as *Tanakh*. You can look at the major divisions of the
Jewish canon and see why: it's an acronym for the three sections.
T is for *Torah*, N for *Nevi'im*, and K for *Ketuvim*. The consonant
sounds T + N + K pronounced together become *Tanakh*.

Of course, in Jesus' day nobody walked around with a neatly
bound copy of *Tanakh* tucked under their arm. The sacred
writings were separate scrolls in those days and too expensive for

---

[35] "'And I, Daniel, alone saw the vision, but the men who were with me did
not see the vision. But a great quaking fell upon them, and they fled into
hiding.' Who were these men? Said Rabbi Yirmiyah, and some say it was
Rabbi Chiya bar Abba, 'They were the [prophets] Chaggai, Zechariah and
Malachi. They were superior to him [Daniel], and he was superior to them.
They were superior to him, in that they were prophets and he wasn't. He was
superior to them, in that he saw the vision and they did not.'" *Talmud*, Tractate
*Megillah* 3a, discussing Daniel 10:7.

most private citizens to own. But Jewish students memorized huge tracts of the scriptures regardless, and Jewish scholars quoted it to each other accurately and often. *Tanakh* was fully authoritative in their world, even in its inconvenient form.

And now, a short trip into linguistics.

Linguists explain that it is common in most languages for things to be referred to by terms that specify only a part of the whole thing being intended, or sometimes that specify a larger or related thing. In American English, for example, we might talk about a battalion or regiment of soldiers as "boots on the ground." We don't mean the boots, we mean the soldiers wearing the boots. We regularly say things like "Philly lost by two touchdowns," and nobody needs the explanation that "Philly" is short for "Philadelphia" and that we don't mean the entire city of Philadelphia but rather the Eagles, the American football team that calls Philadelphia its home. We talk about things done by "the White House" meaning the President, who lives and works in the White House, just as the British speak of "the Crown" when they mean the Queen or "Downing Street" when they mean the Prime Minister, who works at 10 Downing Street.

Or, there's charming shorthand in my hometown of Pittsburgh where we name one of a category and then refer to the rest of the category by saying "'n'at", which is short for "and that (sort of thing)." So a local beer distributor who also sells pretzels and soft drinks goes by the name, "Beer 'N'At," a store that sells electronic game machines and their accessories is "Games 'N'At," and so on.

In the field of linguistics, these sorts of shorthand references go by the names "metonymy" ("meh TAWN uh mee") or "synecdoche" ("sin EK doh kee"); "metonymy" when the word being used is merely related to the thing being referenced, "synecdoche" when the word being used is actually part of the thing being referenced. "The White House" is metonymy when referring to the President; "boots on the ground" is synecdoche when referring to soldiers.

I'm bringing up these technical terms because the New Testament writers used this sort of shorthand in places that are relevant to our topic here. In particular, Jews in the New Testament apparently referred to "the Law and the Prophets" when what they actually meant was the Law, the Prophets, and the Writings—the entire canon of Jewish scripture, otherwise known as *Tanakh*. It appears to have been common shorthand in their culture, an instance of synecdoche.

The place in the New Testament where this becomes clearest is at the very end of Luke's gospel. In Luke 24, Cleopas and an unnamed disciple were walking toward Emmaus when they encountered the risen Jesus, Whom they did not recognize. They told Him their view of the crucifixion and resurrection, at which point He spoke up:

> And he said to them, "O foolish ones, and slow of heart to believe all that the prophets have spoken! Was it not necessary that the Christ should suffer these things and enter into his glory?" And beginning with Moses and all the Prophets, he interpreted to them in all the Scriptures the things concerning himself.[36]

Notice from where Jesus was explaining things. He started in the Torah ("beginning with Moses") and proceeded through *Nevi'im* ("and all the Prophets"). But it appears that He was referring to the entire Jewish canon when it says that He interpreted things in "all the Scriptures" concerning Himself. Jesus was quoting them passages from *Tanakh* that described the Messiah, and He was probably reciting passages from the Psalms and from Daniel (who was not a prophet, remember?) in addition to those from the Prophets and the Torah, and possibly from other places as well.

---

[36] Luke 24:25-27

Then at the end of the same chapter, Jesus suddenly appeared among the Eleven and some others in a locked room. First He reassured them that He was real, alive, and physical. He continued:

> "These are my words that I spoke to you while I was still with you, that everything written about me in the Law of Moses and the Prophets and the Psalms must be fulfilled." Then he opened their minds to understand the Scriptures, and said to them, "Thus it is written, that the Christ should suffer and on the third day rise from the dead, and that repentance for the forgiveness of sins should be proclaimed in his name to all nations, beginning from Jerusalem.[37]

Here Jesus used a variant of the same shorthand: "the Law of Moses" meaning Torah and "the Prophets" meaning *Nevi'im*. We can infer that "the Psalms" was standing in for the rest of the writings, *Ketuvim*, because what He opened their minds to understand was "the Scriptures." "The Law of Moses and the Prophets and the Psalms" most likely referred to *Tanakh*.

Similar uses of the phrase occur in Matthew 7:12, Matthew 11:13, Matthew 22:40, Luke 16:16, Luke 16:29 and 31, John 1:45, Acts 24:14, Acts 26:22, Acts 28:23, and Romans 3:21.

I want to pay special attention to Paul's use of the phrase in Romans 3:

> But now apart from the Law the righteousness of God has been manifested, being witnessed by the Law and the Prophets...[38]

---

[37] Luke 24:44-47

[38] Romans 3:21, *New American Standard Bible*, The Lockman Foundation, Copyright© 1960, 1962, 1963, 1968, 1971, 1972, 1973, 1975, 1977, 1995. I use the NASB here because it translates the sentence literally, word for word. The ESV translators did not appear to understand that Paul's two repetitions of "the Law" were references to two different things, and their rendering obscures Paul's meaning, in my opinion.

Paul said that righteousness from God has been manifested "apart from the Law." But then he said that "the Law and the Prophets" bear witness to that righteousness. He was making a clear distinction. The Law in the first clause is *halakha*, the entire legal system with its explanations of how to carry out the commands of God in the Torah. Paul's assessment, which he discussed in chapter 3 of Romans and summarized in Romans 3:20, was that nobody would be justified before God simply by practicing that system.[39] "The Law and the Prophets" in the second clause is *Tanakh*, which predicts how Jesus would restore God's plan of redemption and testifies clearly to God's righteousness. This passage shows how Paul thought of the two as separate but related. Although he understood that *halakha* with its scrupulous rules and traditions could not produce the character that God desired in His people, Paul believed that *Tanakh*, "the Law and the Prophets," taught an accurate picture of God's true character and the specifics of His plan to rescue the nations.

## The Law of God

Paul and Jesus both argued for the existence of a higher law, a law that "was from the beginning" and which apparently reflects God's character. I have looked for the origin of this line of thinking in the writings of the Rabbis and cannot find it. I think it might have been original to Jesus and His Apostles, though apparently there are ideas similar to it in the writings of the Greek philosopher, Plato.

The higher law of God was the point of Jesus' ministry. Even if Israel had kept the Law, *halakha* could not produce the sort of righteousness that God had always intended for humans to exhibit. Jesus came to establish a kingdom on earth that

---

[39] Romans 3:20 summarizes a complex argument that began back in Romans 2:1, the whole point of which was to demonstrate that simply being Jewish was no guarantee that one had pleased God.

accurately reflected the heart of His Father, an expression of righteousness that was beyond what the Rabbis taught.

This idea about God's true character appears in several places in the New Testament, most notably in I Corinthians 9 and in Romans 7 and 8. While explaining to the Corinthians his job as an Apostle, Paul said this:

> For though I am free from all, I have made myself a servant to all, that I might win more of them. To the Jews I became as a Jew, in order to win Jews. To those under the law I became as one under the law (**though not being myself under the law**) that I might win those under the law. To those outside the law I became as one outside the law (**not being outside the law of God but under the law of Christ**) that I might win those outside the law…I have become all things to all people, that by all means I might save some.[40]

It seems unlikely to me that Paul meant that he stopped practicing *halakha* when he wasn't among Jews, but pretended to practice it while he was among them; that might have been hypocritical of him and might have ended up offending both Jews and non-Jews. It's more likely that he was talking about how he reasoned with these different groups, arguing with each using their own understanding of the Law as a basis for his argument.[41]

But however we take that, Paul went out of his way to assure them that even when *halakha* was not in the picture there was still a higher law that he recognized:

> …not being outside the law of God but under the law of Christ…

To Paul there was a higher law of God that filled the universe. Because God was eternal, His law was eternal. Because God was

---

[40] I Corinthians 9:19-21, 22b, emphasis mine.

[41] Nanos, Mark, *Reading Paul within Judaism: Collected Essays of Mark D. Nanos*, vol 1, Eugene, OR, Cascade Books, 2017, chapter 1.

everywhere, His law was everywhere. Paul called himself "under the law of Christ" because by submitting himself to the Christ and walking in the Holy Spirit, he was able to carry out God's true intention and fulfill God's eternal law.[42]

By Paul's description in Romans 8:38-39 and I Corinthians 13, the chief characteristic of this Law is love. He mentioned it also in Romans 13:8-10. The Apostle John added his "Amen" in I John 4:7-8, as did the Apostle James in James 2:8. Judaism was fully aware of the obligation to love one's neighbor, but not all Jews recognized this as the primary feature of God's character, nor did they all understand how love was to affect their conduct.

Paul believed that the truth about this higher law was available to everyone. He made this clear when he explained to the Romans how nobody has any excuse for wicked behavior:

> For the wrath of God is revealed from heaven against all ungodliness and unrighteousness of men, who by their unrighteousness suppress the truth. For what can be known about God is plain to them, because God has shown it to them. For his invisible attributes, namely, his eternal power and divine nature, have been clearly perceived, ever since the creation of the world, in the things that have been made. So they are without excuse.[43]

A little further on in chapter two of his letter to the Romans, Paul talked about the consciences of Gentiles either condemning or affirming their conduct.[44] To Paul, everybody, even Gentiles, knew the true law of God because it was written in creation and it was written in their consciences.

---

[42] I've just summarized chapters 6 through 8 of Paul's letter to the Romans. Paul also discussed the law of God in that passage, in 7:22, 7:25, 8:4, and 8:7.

[43] Romans 1:18-20

[44] Romans 2:15

Jesus also made reference to an overarching, eternal law. He brought it up explicitly when discussing divorce with some of the Pharisees in Matthew 19. In response to what seemed to them to be an overly strict interpretation they asked Him why He thought Moses allowed them to obtain divorces at all.

> He said to them, "Because of your hardness of heart Moses allowed you to divorce your wives, but from the beginning it was not so."[45]

"From the beginning it was not so." Jesus was pointing out a difference between what Moses wrote in the Torah and what God had intended all along. If we catch His meaning, we know that Moses' law was never intended to be the perfect law for all time, but was instead just a concession to the weakness of a Bronze Age culture: "Because of your hardness of heart..."

Jesus recognized a higher law that was "from the beginning." This higher law, which Paul referred to as "the law of God" in I Corinthians 9, radiates from God's character. This is the law of right and wrong that all humans are born able to recognize in their consciences. It is also the standard by which God will judge all humans at the end of all things, as Paul explained in Romans 2. It could no more pass away than God, Himself, could pass away, because it expresses Himself.

## So What Will Never Pass Away, Again?

So, what was it that Jesus said would never pass away? Well, I've just said that the eternal law of God that emanates from His character will never pass away. But now it's time to revisit that cryptic statement from the beginning of Rabbi Jesus' Sermon on the Mount, because now we can gather what He was talking about.

---

[45] Matthew 19:8

> Do not think that I have come to abolish the Law or the
> Prophets; I have not come to abolish them but to fulfill them.[46]

What Jesus did not come to abolish was "the Law or the
Prophets." When His audience heard "Law" and "Prophets" in
the same phrase, they would have taken it as a reference to
*Tanakh*, the Jewish scriptures. He was (and is) going to fulfill
what was written there. He was not talking about *halakha*, that
entire, complex religious system, at all.

"Fulfill" is a word used by Torah scholars to mean "to teach
accurately or properly." A concept taught inaccurately, dismissed
as irrelevant, or undermined by an incorrect teaching on another
subject, these scholars would say had been "abolished" or
"destroyed."[47] So Jesus, Himself a scholar of Torah, was really
saying in Matthew 5:17, "I'm going to show you what *Tanakh*
really means."

In other words, He was saying that He had come to reveal the
genuine heart of God, the Law as God had intended from the
beginning for humans to practice it, as it was revealed in *Tanakh*.

Let's go on:

> For truly, I say to you, until heaven and earth pass away, not
> an iota, not a dot, will pass from the Law until all is
> accomplished. Therefore whoever relaxes one of the least of
> these commandments and teaches others to do the same will
> be called least in the kingdom of heaven, but whoever does
> them and teaches them will be called great in the kingdom of
> heaven.[48]

---

[46] Matthew 5:17

[47] Vander Laan, Ray, op. cit.

[48] Matthew 5:18-19

First of all, notice the time frame. "Until heaven and earth pass away" is very specific; He was referring to Isaiah 65:17, in which the Almighty says:

> For behold, I create new heavens
> and a new earth,
> and the former things shall not be remembered
> or come into mind.

Whatever it was that Jesus was declaring here would not change at any time during the age before God the Almighty has created the new heaven and Earth. Have you seen a new Earth yet? In chapter four I will explain how Jesus planted the kingdom of God and began this creation of a new Earth, but He has not completed it yet. So I infer that we're still in the period that Jesus was talking about. "Until all is accomplished" was His goal, not His time frame. It referred to what Jesus is going to carry out before "heaven and Earth pass away." He is going to fulfill all that is written in *Tanakh*.

And He is still doing just that. Many prophecies have been fulfilled completely, others partially; and still others, like Isaiah 25:6-8 which was quoted by Paul in I Corinthians 15:54, will be fulfilled in the future. And of course, Jesus' work in redemption fulfills more than just prophetic predictions, but fulfills God's entire plan as laid out in *Tanakh*. This is well underway but will be completed only when He returns.

Next, let me explain Jesus' hyperbole. The English Standard Version gives us the Greek versions: "not an iota, not a dot." Iota is a Greek letter. Jesus was more likely referring to the Hebrew letter *yod*, the smallest letter in the Hebrew alphabet, and then to *taagin*, the tiny embellishments at the edges of the letters in Hebrew scribal copies of the Torah. *Yod* looks like this: י.

Jesus said that none of those letters or pen strokes will pass from "the Law," and that whoever wants to be called great in the kingdom of heaven "does [these commandments] and teaches them." But He had already established his topic, which was *Tanakh*. "Law" in this case has to be synecdoche for the topic he already specified, shorthand for what He had said in the previous sentence—Law, Prophets, and Writings. So He was neither endorsing *halakha* nor recommending the five books of Moses in this case, He was endorsing *Tanakh*, just as He had in the previous verse. In effect He was saying that we need to pay close attention to the plan of redemption that God revealed throughout the scriptures and also to the character He revealed as a model for our own conduct.

And notice that those who relax the commandments in *Tanakh* will be called least "*in* the kingdom of heaven." He was not talking about something that would exclude them from membership in the kingdom of God. He was talking about members of that kingdom who teach *Tanakh* incorrectly or dismiss parts of it. They won't be punished, but they will be considered of lesser honor than those who recognized and taught *Tanakh* properly. Salvation is not at stake here; rank is.

Jesus finally brought up *halakha*, the Jewish religious system, at the end of the paragraph:

> For I tell you, unless your righteousness exceeds that of the scribes and Pharisees, you will never enter the kingdom of heaven.[49]

This referred to the concentrated study of the written laws of the *Torah*, the instructions of the Oral Law that appeared later in the *Mishna*, the explanations from the Rabbis that appeared later in the *Gemara*, and whatever other rabbinic *midrashim* were already in their culture. Those were the means by which the scribes and Pharisees pursued righteousness. And Jesus' assessment of their pursuit was clear: it was not good enough to get His *talmidim* into the kingdom of heaven.

---

[49] Matthew 5:20

In short, Jesus was saying exactly what Paul was saying in Romans 3:21: *Tanakh* bears witness to God's character, but practicing *halakha* as the Jews practiced it would not produce that sort of character.

He was also saying, though, that His *talmidim* needed to read and learn *Tanakh* and discern from it the character of God so they could behave like Him, as part of their activity within the kingdom of heaven. Jesus had done this Himself, and it was reflected in His teaching when He spoke of God's character in the Sermon on the Mount.

We're ready now to dive into the sermon itself.

# Chapter 4: The Kingdom of Heaven in the Jewish Mind

## Outline of the Sermon on the Mount

**Subject: Life in the Kingdom of God**

I. God wants you to model His character... — Matthew 5
- A. Ordinary believers are holy — (5:3-12)
- B. Your job is to demonstrate God's character — (5:13-16)
- C. The scriptures are your guide — (5:17-20)
- D. God's character is your standard
  1. Hold relationships in highest esteem — (5:21-26)
  2. Keep your desires ordinate — (5:27-30)
  3. Speak truth at all times — (5:31-37)
  4. Do good to all, not evil — (5:38-48)

II. ...so give Him your whole-hearted devotion... — Matthew 6-7:2
- A. Serve God, not reputation — (6:1-18)
- B. Serve God, not wealth — (6:19-24)
- C. Serve God, not self — (6:25-7:2)

III. ...and He will produce His character in you. — Matthew 7:3-27
- A. Stay humble — (7:3-6)
- B. Pray for God's help — (7:7-12)
- C. Be diligent — (7:13-14)
- D. Stick to the Master's training — (7:15-23)
- E. He will make you unshakable — (7:24-27)

And he opened his mouth and taught them, saying:

"Blessed are the poor in spirit, for theirs is the kingdom of heaven...

"Blessed are those who are persecuted for righteousness' sake, for theirs is the kingdom of heaven.[1]

---

[1] Matthew 5:2-3, 10

I was wrong when I thought that Jesus did not announce the subject of His sermon. There it is, right up front and bracketing the Beatitudes: the kingdom of heaven.

"Heaven" in this case was a substitute for saying "God." Jews, then and now, avoid saying "God" or using His name. Modern Jews, when we encounter the holy Name יְהֹוָה while reading the *Torah* or prayers aloud, will substitute the word "*adonai*," which is Hebrew for "Lord," or "*ha shem*," which is Hebrew for "the Name," or sometimes combine those two as "*adoshem*," which is just a made-up word combining the Hebrew for "Lord" and "name." We've been doing it so long that nobody knows anymore how the Name is supposed to be pronounced.[2] Gentiles may say "Yahweh," "Yahveh," or "Jehovah", but we have no way to tell if any of those are correct. The commandment says "the Lord will not hold him guiltless who takes His name in vain,"[3] and the sages reasoned that if you never say it, you can't take it in vain.[4] So the phrase "kingdom of heaven" in Matthew's gospel was just a very Jewish way of saying "kingdom of God."

I don't think I'm stretching things when I say that the kingdom of God was the topic of Jesus' public ministry. From the very beginning He was announcing the arrival of "the kingdom of heaven" or "the kingdom of God." Matthew said it was the message that Jesus preached once He settled in Galilee.[5] Mark said the same: "Now after John was arrested, Jesus came into

---

[2] The vowel markings in יְהֹוָה specify a pronunciation something like "y'h'VAH," but those markings were added by the Masoretes sometime between the 5th and 10th centuries CE, so we don't know if they're correct.

[3] Exodus 20:7, Deuteronomy 5:11

[4] The foolishness of using God's name for no reason is discussed generally in *Talmud*, Tractate *T'murah* 3b, but the inference "Just don't say the Name and you'll be safe" was drawn later and external to that discussion. Whether that's really a good way to avoid what God was talking about when He issued the third of the Ten Commandments is another topic, one that I will cover in chapter nine when I talk about the false prophets mentioned in Matthew 7. I'll give away the game, though; I don't think it is.

[5] Matthew 4:17

Galilee, proclaiming the gospel of God, and saying, 'The time is fulfilled, and the kingdom of God is at hand; repent and believe in the gospel.'"[6]

Luke's gospel said the same in the form of a story. Luke described an incident in which Jesus, participating in the weekly Torah service in his hometown of Nazareth, read a passage from Isaiah chapter 61 that describes a chief characteristic of the kingdom of heaven, namely that all the needs of God's people are met with His favor.[7] The passage identifies this with the year of Jubilee.

The heart of the modern, weekly Torah service consists of reading publicly a passage from the Torah broken into several pieces, followed by a reading from the prophets called the *haftarah* portion.[8] This passage in Luke where Jesus read Isaiah in the synagogue is the earliest mention in historical documents of anything like the modern *haftarah* reading, and there is no other information clarifying how the practice worked back then. We don't know, for instance, whether the *haftarah* portion occurred on a schedule or whether Jesus was permitted to select his own portion. However, the Nazarenes were probably showing Jesus their esteem by letting him read the *haftarah* portion; it was an honor. It's also likely that the portion was longer than the mere two verses mentioned in Luke's gospel; I'm guessing that He read the entire chapter.

Jesus followed this reading with a comment that upset his listeners: "Today this Scripture has been fulfilled in your hearing."[9] They took Him to mean that He was claiming to be someone special. He was interpreting the special time of God's

---

[6] Mark 1:14-15

[7] Luke 4:16-30, quoting Isaiah 61:1-2.

[8] *Haftarah* means "taking leave" or "parting." In this context it refers to leaving the Torah reading and moving on to the reading of the prophets.

[9] Luke 4:21b

favor mentioned Isaiah 61 as the imminent arrival of God's kingdom, and declaring that it was arriving along with Him.

In all of the gospel accounts of Jesus' early ministry, what Jesus was saying about the kingdom of heaven was that it was arriving. Saying specifically "the time is fulfilled" as He did in Mark's gospel, or saying "This passage is being fulfilled as we speak" as He did in Luke's gospel, tells us that we're reading it correctly if we think that He was saying "It's arriving any day now."

## The Promise Is For You

And then it arrived.

After Jesus rose from the dead, the author of Acts told us that Jesus remained with his Apostles for forty days, talking to them about the kingdom of God,[10] presumably because that's what they were about to experience. Then, on the day of Pentecost when the Holy Spirit fell on the disciples, Peter stood up and announced to the crowd what was happening:

> …this is what was uttered through the prophet Joel:
>
> 'And in the last days it shall be, God declares,
> that I will pour out my Spirit on all flesh,
> and your sons and your daughters shall prophesy,
> and your young men shall see visions,
> and your old men shall dream dreams…'[11]

His reference to Joel's prophecy gave his audience reason to connect all the prophecies from *Tanakh* concerning what would happen "in the last days" to what was beginning there in Jerusalem. So did Jesus' use of Isaiah 61 to describe what was beginning while He was ministering among them.[12] That's quite a

---

[10] Acts 1:1-3

[11] Acts 2:16b-17

[12] Luke 4:16-30

large body of predictions containing some astonishing things that we'll get to in a moment.

Peter continued in the same vein when the hearers asked what they ought to do:

> Repent and be baptized every one of you in the name of Jesus Christ for the forgiveness of your sins, and you will receive the gift of the Holy Spirit. For the promise is for you and for your children and for all who are far off, everyone whom the Lord our God calls to himself.[13]

Pay particular attention to the words, "the promise is for you." What promise was that? Where in *Tanakh* does one see a promise of a gift of the Holy Spirit, and to what was Peter connecting that gift?

Joel's prophecy that Peter had just quoted leaps to mind. Isaiah 59:21 also comes to mind, where Adonai says "My Spirit that is upon you, and my words that I have put in your mouth, shall not depart out of your mouth, or out of the mouth of your offspring, [forever]." And Ezekiel 39:29 speaks of the last days in which "I will not hide my face anymore from them, when I pour out my Spirit upon the house of Israel…"

However, to the Jews there was really only one promise worth mentioning: the promise to Abraham. That was *the* promise. Their entire nation, their sense of destiny and purpose in the Almighty, and their expectation of great things in the future were all built on God's promise to their faithful forefather:

> "I will bless those who bless you, and him who dishonors you I will curse, and in you all the families of the earth shall be blessed."[14]

---

[13] Acts 2:38b-39

[14] Genesis 12:3

In fact, Peter's audience at Pentecost would have considered all the predictions in the prophecies in *Tanakh* to be fulfillment of God's primary promise to Abraham. Peter's audience would have heard him connecting the outpouring of the Holy Spirit, described in Joel's prophecy concerning "the latter days" and being performed right before their eyes, with the fulfillment of the central promise to the Jewish nation. The Holy Spirit falling on "all flesh" was the beginning of the fulfillment of God's promise to Abraham, in which all the Gentiles would be blessed. The blessing was to go out to all that God would call from every nation, not just to the Jews: "...all who are far off, everyone whom the Lord our God calls to himself."[15]

The promises among the prophets included restoration of Israel's nation, the Twelve Tribes being reunited under the Messiah King, idolatry and apostasy being removed from Israel by the grace of God, the abolition of war, the removal of all curses, the removal of the wicked from among the righteous, the exaltation of the Law and the Temple in the sight of all the Gentiles...

To put it concisely, Peter was talking about what Jews saw as The End of All Things. Only, it seemed to be occurring in the middle of all things.[16]

This is the mystery of God's kingdom inaugurated through the death and resurrection of the Messiah: the end has begun, but the manifestation of God's kingdom will continue to grow and increase until it is finally completed. Jesus was planting a seed; but from that seed was to grow a tree that would dominate the garden of God's planting.[17] It was leaven that was supposed eventually to leaven everything.[18] It was salt that was supposed to

---

[15] Acts 2:17

[16] That turn of phrase, "the end of all things ...occurring in the middle of all things," I borrowed from NT Wright in his book, *What Saint Paul Really Said,* op. cit.

[17] Matthew 13:31-32, Mark 4:31-32, Luke 13:19

[18] Matthew 13:33, Luke 13:21

season the earth.[19] It was light that was supposed to illuminate the world.[20]

And don't miss the fact that it was the fulfillment of Judaism, not its replacement.[21]

But all of this was still in the future when Jesus preached on the hillside. Jesus apparently knew that the purpose of His ministry was to initiate the kingdom of God which would end in the fulfillment of the promise to Israel and of the predictions of the restoration of Israel in the last days. His purpose in training His disciples, then, while planting the seed of the kingdom of God, was to explain to them and to us what life in the kingdom was supposed to be like while this process of growing the kingdom was ongoing.

## Kingdom Basics in Prophecy

There were a lot of different interpretations of the Jewish prophecies among Second Temple Jews. It would be an enormous task to catalog them all, and honestly I wouldn't know where to start if I wanted to. However, there are several cultural elements about the kingdom that were so fundamental that virtually everybody would have had them in their thinking somewhere, regardless of how they interpreted the prophecies.

Here in the United States, when cartoonists want to represent heaven for some reason, they will draw puffy, white clouds as seen from above, and on those clouds will be standing men holding ancient, Greek harps and wearing long, white robes. Some of them might have wings like those of a dove sticking out

---

[19] Matthew 5:13

[20] Matthew 5:14-16

[21] For a more complete discussion of the gospel events fulfilling the calling of Israel, see Wright, NT, *How God Became King: the Forgotten Story of the Gospels*, New York, HarperCollins Publishers, 2012, chapter 4.

from their shoulder blades. Often there will be a grey-bearded man overseeing them, sometimes standing behind a lectern and deciding whether and on what terms they may enter a gate; that will be St. Peter. Most of those details come from overly literal interpretations of things in the Bible. Practically nobody really believes that heaven is going to look like this. Still, any American looking at the drawing will immediately recognize it as a cartoon depiction of heaven. Those elements in the drawing—clouds, robes, harps, wings, St. Peter—are things that nearly all Americans recognize.

In similar fashion, Jews from the earliest times through the first century CE shared some common notions about what was in heaven and how it would become part of their experience when heaven touched earth. Their version seems to have included a place where God and man walked together, a well-watered garden with rivers and trees, a high mountain in the far north, the Tree of Life, and eventually a heavenly version of Jerusalem and its temple. There were all sorts of interpretations of prophecies that differed dramatically from each other, but the few items I just mentioned were in the "cartoon" version that all the Jews would have recognized as the kingdom of heaven.

So let's take a walking tour of *Tanakh* and pick out some of the things it says about those elements. They will help us imagine what might have been in the minds of the *talmidim* to whom Jesus was describing the kingdom of heaven. We will see that they carried these forward into the New Testament and used them to describe what Jesus established.

We should start with Eden. In Genesis 2:5-15 the writer described Earth in the process of creation. God created Man from the dirt outside of Eden (2:7 and 3:23), and then God planted the garden. It was in the east, a specific location that was not the entire earth (2:8). It contained two important trees: the tree of life and the tree of knowledge of good and evil (2:9). Out of Eden flowed rivers that watered the earth (2:10-14). Associated with those rivers were gold and precious stones (2:11-12). Man's job was to tend the garden (2:15); but that was probably secondary to Man's primary job of subduing the rest of the earth (1:28). Most importantly, God and Man walked together in Eden (3:8).

Eden was the garden of God, as we'll see from other passages in a moment. It represented a perfect situation for Man in which Man and God were together. When Man tending the perfect garden gets combined with Man subduing the rest of the earth, it suggests that God's intention was that Man was to make the rest of the earth like Eden—as in heaven, so on earth.[22]

After Man fell, Man and God were estranged, and Man was no longer permitted in Eden. God's desire from that point forward, in the Jewish mind, would have been to re-establish the intimacy of Eden, God and Man together, and for Man to return to his intended role, making the earth look like heaven.

Eden made another appearance in Ezekiel 28. Ezekiel 28 is one of two passages in *Tanakh* where a particular ancient story played a role, a story about a cherub of high station in heaven who tried to exalt himself above God, only to be cast down to the earth and humiliated before men. The passage in Ezekiel 28 is actually about the King of Tyre; but the writer used the ancient story of the fallen cherub as a metaphor to describe the king's sin and its results. The cherub story was apparently well-enough embedded in the Hebrew culture that the writer could use it as a metaphor without having to explain himself to his readers, the way that twenty-first century Americans can use bits of *The Princess Bride* or other popular movies to lampoon things without having to explain. ("You keep using that word. I don't think it means what you think it means.")

---

[22] Heiser, Michael S., *The Unseen Realm*, Lexham Press, Bellingham, WA, 2015, p. 51. The echo of Jesus' recitation of the Lord's Prayer, Matthew 6:10, is deliberate.

We know it was about Eden because the writer said so. He called it a lament about the King of Tyre (Ezekiel 28:12), but then the prophet said to him, "You were in Eden, the garden of God..." (v13). The King of Tyre was not likely to have been in the Garden of God; the prophet was comparing him to the cherub who fell. He went on to name several elements of Eden, calling it "the holy mountain of God" where God and the cherubs lived together (v14), and describing the precious stones that were assigned to the cherub (v13).

We can pick up a few more elements of this place where God and His heavenly creatures met from the other passage that uses the same, ancient story, which is Isaiah 14. Isaiah 14 is about a King of Babylon, but again, the writer used the story of the fallen cherub as a metaphor to describe the condition of the King. In Isaiah 14:13, the writer called Eden "the mount of assembly in the far reaches of the north" and described the various other beings in God's council as "the stars of God" in the heavens, echoing a similar mention in Job 38:4-7.[23]

Let's list the elements in this picture of heaven on earth that occurred in these three descriptions of Eden. We're going to see these things elsewhere as we move forward:

- God and other heavenly beings walked with Man there;

- The Tree of Life was there;

- Gold and precious stones were there;

- It was the mountain of assembly;

- It was well-watered and lush;

---

[23] I encounter lots of Protestant Christians who have difficulty accepting that there's any being in heaven besides God, Himself. When I mention other heavenly beings, they reply "There is only one God!" That's not the point, though. The Bible is full of other beings for whom what we call "heaven" is apparently home: cherubs, seraphs, angels, "sons of God," and so forth. Clearly those are created beings. Just as clearly, God created them, and did so before He created us and our Earth. I'm not sure why this is controversial.

- It was in the east (but also in the far reaches of the north!)

Let me re-emphasize: this is not a list of things that Jews literally believed about Eden or about heaven. Just as Americans recognize clouds, harps, robes and wings as "heaven" in their minds but don't usually think that heaven is actually like that, this is a list of cultural cues that had been repeated often enough that all Jews of those periods, upon hearing those things, would recognize them as a description of Eden, and therefore as a description of heaven coming to earth and of man and God being reunited.

That's why it was possible for "in the east" and "in the far reaches of the north" to be true about the same thing. Don't think of them as literal directions; think of them as code words triggering their thoughts about the home of God. In Canaanite and Ugaritic mythology, "the mountains in the far north" was apparently thought to be the place where the gods lived, and there are reasons to think that their neighbors, the Hebrews, borrowed some of their expressions about this.[24]

An instance of this usage occurs in Psalm 48:1b-2:

> His holy mountain, beautiful in elevation,
> is the joy of all the earth,
> Mount Zion, in the far north,
> the city of the great King.

If you take a look at a map of Jerusalem that shows the location of Mt. Zion, you'll see that it's not on the north side of the old city, it's toward the south. Nor is Jerusalem, itself, in the north of Israel; it's a little south of center. Nor is Zion much of a mountain; it's more like a hill. "North" and "elevation" in this case were not physical locations or descriptions but a reference to Zion's connection with the divine, a link between the Holy of Holies in the temple and the Almighty God who appeared there.

---

[24] Heiser, *The Unseen Realm*, op. cit., chapter 6.

The important point here is to notice how the Hebrew psalmist associated Mt. Zion, the location of the temple in Jerusalem, with the mount of assembly, the place where God and Man met together in Eden. In Hebrew religion God and Man met together in the Holy of Holies, the inner chamber of the temple on Mt. Zion; that's apparently what was left to the Jews of the intimacy of Eden. But they were clearly hoping for more in the future, as we'll see.

As the messages of the prophets began accumulating in Jewish religion, they called on these same images and sometimes added to them. Near the beginning of Isaiah's prophecy, we're told:

> It shall come to pass in the latter days
> that the mountain of the house of the Lord
> shall be established as the highest of the mountains,
> and shall be lifted up above the hills;
> and all the nations shall flow to it,
> and many peoples shall come, and say:
> "Come, let us go up to the mountain of the Lord,
> to the house of the God of Jacob,
> that he may teach us his ways
> and that we may walk in his paths."
> For out of Zion shall go forth the law,
> and the word of the Lord from Jerusalem.
> He shall judge between the nations,
> and shall decide disputes for many peoples;
> and they shall beat their swords into plowshares,
> and their spears into pruning hooks;
> nation shall not lift up sword against nation,
> neither shall they learn war anymore.[25]

I doubt that there will be tectonic shifting causing Mt. Zion to rise above all other mountains on Earth, although, candidly, that's not impossible, God could actually choose to do that. I do, however, believe that the prophet was predicting the rise of the

---

[25] Isaiah 2:2-4, Micah 4:1-4

God of Israel in a way that will cause the Gentiles to recognize their need for His wisdom, for which reason they will come to Him and accept His guidance. According to Isaiah, that resort to the God of Jacob will produce world peace.

We're looking at elements of heaven on Earth appearing in Hebrew prophecies of a future restoration. The connection here is the mountain of YHWH, now associated with Mt. Zion, and further associated with the temple: "the house of the God of Jacob."

Mt. Zion is in Jerusalem, of course, so Jerusalem became part of the reference. Isaiah set the context for our next prophecy in Isaiah 24:23, where he wrote:

> Then the moon will be confounded
> and the sun ashamed,
> for the Lord of hosts reigns
> on Mount Zion and in Jerusalem,
> and his glory will be before his elders.

That setting still applies when we reach Isaiah 25:6-8:

> On this mountain the Lord of hosts will make for all peoples
> a feast of rich food, a feast of well-aged wine,
> of rich food full of marrow, of aged wine well refined.
> And he will swallow up on this mountain
> the covering that is cast over all peoples,
> the veil that is spread over all nations.
> He will swallow up death forever;
> and the Lord God will wipe away tears from all faces,
> and the reproach of his people he will take away from all the
>     earth,
> for the Lord has spoken.

Here the mountain of YHWH becomes the place where death will be swallowed up and all tears will be wiped away, a picture repeated by Paul, the Apostle in I Corinthians 15:54. It will be for all peoples, not just Jews. But it was not just on the mountain of

God that this would happen; now the prophecy included the city, Jerusalem.

And notice, back in Isaiah chapter 24, how the sun and moon will be "ashamed," or overshadowed, presumably by God Himself. We see that again when we get to Isaiah 60, where the entire chapter describes the restoration of Israel as an enormous influx of wealth, the wealth of the Gentiles.

> Your gates shall be open continually;
> day and night they shall not be shut,
> that people may bring to you the wealth of the nations,
> with their kings led in procession.[26]

The description of the wealth flowing from Gentile kings into Jerusalem, and in particular into God's temple, goes on for almost twenty verses, then the prophet says:

> I will make your overseers peace
> and your taskmasters righteousness.
> Violence shall no more be heard in your land,
> devastation or destruction within your borders;
> you shall call your walls Salvation,
> and your gates Praise.
> The sun shall be no more
> your light by day,
> nor for brightness shall the moon
> give you light;
> but the Lord will be your everlasting light,
> and your God will be your glory.[27]

By this time the image of heaven on earth contained peace, righteousness, salvation, and praise in addition to wealth and dominion over the nations. And it was repeated: they won't need the sun or the moon for light, because Adonai Himself would be their light. Not only would God walk among them; His glory

---

[26] Isaiah 60:11

[27] Isaiah 60:17b-19

would shine on them continually. It would be even better than Eden.

One more thing: in Isaiah 65, somehow the restoration of Jerusalem on God's holy mountain would result in a new heaven and a new earth:

> For behold, I create new heavens
> and a new earth,
> and the former things shall not be remembered
> or come into mind.
> But be glad and rejoice forever
> in that which I create;
> for behold, I create Jerusalem to be a joy,
> and her people to be a gladness...[28]

> The wolf and the lamb shall graze together;
> the lion shall eat straw like the ox,
> and dust shall be the serpent's food.
> They shall not hurt or destroy
> in all my holy mountain,"
> says the Lord.[29]

I've only cited the opening and closing verses of this particular portion. Between those points, Isaiah described a world in which nobody wept and nobody died prematurely, there was no calamity nor did anybody labor in vain. That ideal world, Isaiah tied to Jerusalem (v. 18) and to God's holy mountain (v. 25).

Isaiah wrote in the eighth century BCE. Ezekiel, two to three hundred years later, wrote a similar description:

> I will make a covenant of peace with them. It shall be an everlasting covenant with them. And I will set them in their land and multiply them, and will set my sanctuary in their midst forevermore. My dwelling place shall be with them,

---

[28] Isaiah 65:17-18

[29] Isaiah 65:25

and I will be their God, and they shall be my people. Then the nations will know that I am the Lord who sanctifies Israel, when my sanctuary is in their midst forevermore.[30]

Ezekiel repeated the idea of God living among His people again, tying into their images by associating God's presence with His temple: "[I] will set my sanctuary in their midst forevermore." He went on from chapter 40 through the end of the prophecy describing a spiritual temple that was to be theirs at the end of all things.

In visions of God he brought me to the land of Israel, and set me down on a very high mountain, on which was a structure like a city to the south. When he brought me there, behold, there was a man whose appearance was like bronze, with a linen cord and a measuring reed in his hand.[31]

The man went on to measure the city and its temple for the next eight chapters. Notice that Ezekiel identified this as a vision. What he saw sat on a very high mountain which was to the north of a city; this was a temple and a city that exist where God and His heavenly servants live. But it was also in the land of Israel, so it was part of their restoration.

Chapter 47 begins this way:

Then he brought me back to the door of the temple, and behold, water was issuing from below the threshold of the temple toward the east (for the temple faced east)…[32]

The temple faced east because that's where Eden was. In chapter 43 Ezekiel was told that only the Prince, who was a Messianic figure, was permitted to sit there facing east; the right to return to Eden belonged to Messiah.

---

[30] Ezekiel 37:26-28

[31] Ezekiel 40:2-3

[32] Ezekiel 47:1

Chapter 47 goes on:

> Going on eastward with a measuring line in his hand, the man measured a thousand cubits, and then led me through the water, and it was ankle-deep. Again he measured a thousand, and led me through the water, and it was knee-deep. Again he measured a thousand, and led me through the water, and it was waist-deep. Again he measured a thousand, and it was a river that I could not pass through, for the water had risen. It was deep enough to swim in, a river that could not be passed through...[33]

> Then he led me back to the bank of the river. As I went back, I saw on the bank of the river very many trees on the one side and on the other. And he said to me, "This water flows toward the eastern region and goes down into the Arabah, and enters the sea; when the water flows into the sea, the water will become fresh. And wherever the river goes, every living creature that swarms will live, and there will be very many fish... And on the banks, on both sides of the river, there will grow all kinds of trees for food. Their leaves will not wither, nor their fruit fail, but they will bear fresh fruit every month, because the water for them flows from the sanctuary. Their fruit will be for food, and their leaves for healing."[34]

We're back to Eden, but better than Eden: Eden that has the power to feed and heal mankind. From the sanctuary on that heavenly mountain comes the river that waters the earth and makes things live wherever it goes. The trees on either side of the river never fail to provide food, and their leaves provide healing. This is the perfect place, the well-watered garden that the earth was supposed to become under Man's guidance before he fell.

Now, all of these things that I've been listing would have been in the minds of Jesus' students when He introduced His topic as

---

[33] Ezekiel 47:3-5

[34] Ezekiel 47:7-9, 12

"the kingdom of God." Naturally, each of them would have had their own, pet interpretations, but the elements of Eden would have risen in their minds in some form: a watered garden, the mountain of God, the city and temple from which the Law of God leads and ennobles the Gentiles, the Tree of Life that heals and feeds, and above all God walking openly with His people as at the beginning.

You might think that I was guessing about this, but we actually know it. If they did not have these pictures in their minds when Jesus preached the kingdom of God to them the first time, they did by the time the Church was developing. We know this because they wrote it down.

This is how the writer of the letter to the Hebrews described where believers had arrived who had embraced the Christ:

> But you have come to Mount Zion and to the city of the living God, the heavenly Jerusalem, and to innumerable angels in festal gathering, and to the assembly of the firstborn who are enrolled in heaven, and to God, the judge of all, and to the spirits of the righteous made perfect, and to Jesus, the mediator of a new covenant, and to the sprinkled blood that speaks a better word than the blood of Abel.[35]

He stated it plainly: believers had arrived on Mount Zion and in the heavenly Jerusalem. The prophecies from the past were about them, those who embraced Jesus. The promises were for them. The kingdom came.[36]

What's more, every single one of the elements we listed from the prophets appears in John's Apocalypse in the closing chapters.

---

[35] Hebrews 12:22-24

[36] The writer of Hebrews identified some other elements that I haven't spoken of: the assembly of the firstborn, the perfection of the righteous ones, the new covenant, and the blood that speaks better than the blood of Abel. There's a lot more in the prophets and it's worth a great deal of study. I'm just skimming over the surface.

He depicted the heavenly Jerusalem coming down from God, in which God walks with His people and the city needs no lights. Interpreters tend to put all this into some future event, but they actually began when Jesus rose from the dead. We *have come* to the heavenly Jerusalem, said the writer of Hebrews. One can walk through the verses of Revelation 21-22 and point them back to the images of restoration from the prophets.

Just look at how it starts:

> Then I saw a new heaven and a new earth...[37] (compare to Isaiah 65:17)

> And I saw the holy city, new Jerusalem, coming down out of heaven from God...[38] (compare to Ezekiel 40 and following, and to the references to Jerusalem in Isaiah 2, 60, and 65)

> Behold, the dwelling place of God is with man. He will dwell with them...[39] (compare to Eden, especially Genesis 3:8, and to God among His people in Isaiah 60:18-19 and Ezekiel 37:27)

> He will wipe away every tear from their eyes, and death shall be no more...[40] (compare to Isaiah 25:8)

> ...neither shall there be mourning, nor crying, nor pain anymore, for the former things have passed away[41] (compare to Isaiah 25:8 and Isaiah 65:17, 19-20).

I could continue through Revelation 21 and into chapter 22, pointing out the constant connection to the Hebrew prophets. The great, high mountain from Ezekiel is there. The man measuring

---

[37] Revelation 21:1

[38] Revelation 21:2

[39] Revelation 21:3b

[40] Revelation 21:4a

[41] Revelation 21:4b

the city is there. The gold and precious stones from Eden are there. The river of life flowing from beneath the sanctuary is there. The trees that heal and feed are there; they get identified as the Tree of Life, last seen in Eden when Man was driven from the garden.

The Apostles of Jesus recognized that He inaugurated the kingdom of God on earth. The kingdom that He inaugurated is the one described to the Jews through their prophets. The Apostles recognized this and declared to us that it was coming to pass just as it had been predicted in *Tanakh*.

## Where Is It?

So, where is it?

One common answer to this question is that the kingdom of God is in the Church. When we get together to worship Jesus, the Messiah, we declare His coming and celebrate what He established among us who worship His name. However imperfectly we represent His will, when we accept each other as fellow-worshipers of the Messiah we exercise the core principle of the kingdom of heaven, which is to love one another. Moreover, some of us see God healing the sick and delivering people from demonic oppression in the context of our worship, and that, also, reflects the arrival of the kingdom of God. I agree, some of the fulfillment appears there.

Most of us go straight from there to the coming apocalypse at the end of all things; and in fact, some don't even bother with the Church but say that the fulfillment comes entirely in the future. When most of us think of last things, we expect things on our present Earth to continue as they have been, either getting progressively better or worse depending our point of view, until there is some sort of cataclysm in which the Lord will descend from on high, place his feet on the Mount of Olives, defeat massive armies, depose human governments, and establish an everlasting kingdom in which all wrong things are set right.

I partly agree here, too; that cataclysm is certain to happen. As just a fraction of the vast support for this in the New Testament, Jesus told several parables that depicted a landowner going on a journey and leaving servants in charge; in those parables, the landowner always returned, and always judged the performance of those he left in charge.[42] He told other parables of a wealthy man planning a feast; the feast always occurred, and things happened to those involved according to how they handled the invitations and preparations.[43] The judgment by God at the end of the age was very much part of Jewish thought, and very much part of Jesus' teaching.

However, Jesus encouraged His *talmidim* to look for something sooner than that. Jesus said the kingdom would begin as something insignificant, but would gradually grow to dominate its environment. I mentioned this in passing before I started talking about Eden.

Let me remind you:

There are three parables in the middle of Matthew's thirteenth chapter, coming right after the Parable of the Sower, that all speak of this characteristic of the kingdom of heaven. The first is the Parable of the Tares;[44] the second is the Parable of the Mustard Seed;[45] and the third is the Parable of Leaven.[46] All three

---

[42] See Matthew 21:33, Matthew 25:14, Mark 12:1, Mark 13:34, Luke 19:11, Luke 20:9. Some of these can be taken as telling the story of the Jews, and the returning Master was Jesus, Himself, appearing to Israel. But others can be taken as Jesus leaving the disciples in charge of His Church, and then returning to judge them (see especially Matthew 24:44-51). Or perhaps all of them are both.

[43] See Matthew 22:2, Matthew 25:1, Luke 14:15.

[44] Matthew 13:24-30

[45] Matthew 13:31-32

of these parables represent the kingdom of heaven beginning as something small and insignificant. In all three the kingdom gets planted in the presence of other things that are not of the same nature as itself. In all three the growth of the kingdom takes place gradually, out of sight and over time, but at the end the kingdom has come to dominate its surroundings.

We can take these parables to be Jesus' warning that though the kingdom would appear suddenly and full-blown with fanfare at the end of the age, it was also going to appear as something small that would gradually take over. Both were true.

What we're looking for, then, is something arising out of Jesus' ministry through the Church that has gradually made the earth a better place for human beings to live and grow, in some sense has begun to influence the nations positively, and in some sense includes God living among His people.

During the Enlightenment there were thinkers and writers who deliberately based their thoughts on the truths of the Christian faith—men like Blackstone, Burke, Locke, and Jefferson—but there were others, like Spinoza, Voltaire, and Gibbon, who made no bones about their hatred for Christianity. It was the thoughts of these latter writers that filled the books from which most of us learned history. As a result, we have grown up with the notion that the modern world was inevitable because of the foundations built by the Greeks and the Romans, and that if the Church had anything to do with the modern world it was to dig in its heels and do everything in its power to prevent it from happening.

It's taken me nearly forty years of investigating and relearning the history of the West, but I've come to see that that view is nearly the polar opposite of what really happened. What happened, instead, was that Jesus irrevocably changed the world for the better.

---

[46] Matthew 13:33

We don't realize how uniform and impoverished the ancient world was. Prior to the coming of the Messiah, most of world history consisted of a few, powerful warlords marshaling their strength to dominate the multitude of weaker persons in order to enslave them, and then to employ them in building monuments to their greatness. The economies of these ancient empires were remarkably unproductive and the vast majority of the people lived just barely above subsistence level. It was not uncommon for a dying king to take literally thousands of peasants, servants, and courtiers with him into the underworld by killing them. Individuals effectively had no value at all.[47]

Nor do many of us have a good idea by what mechanisms the ancient world became the modern world. We have this odd notion that it was somehow inevitable, but in fact there was little in the ancient world that had much chance of changing the pattern of domination and monument-building.

Prof. Rodney Stark of Baylor University, in his book *How the West Won*, argues that Christianity contained the ideas that lifted humanity out of that dead pattern and created the modern world. He lists quotes from nineteenth century historians declaring how the West descended into darkness for centuries after the fall of Rome—and then explains that twenty-first century historians now regard such statements as a complete fraud. Europeans following the fall of Rome were better-fed, taller, and healthier than their Roman counterparts, and technology, education, commerce, and art thrived in the European world after Rome. Furthermore, he argues, the ideas of Christianity led to the abolition of slavery, the rise of liberal governance, innovation in free commerce, and attention paid to human virtue, all of which gave the West advantages over other civilizations.

He's not alone in saying so. I came across a podcast from a popular show in Britain called *Unbelievable?* in which one of the

---

[47] Stark, Rodney, *How the West Won: the Neglected Story of the Triumph of Modernity*, ISI Books, Wilmington, DE, 2014, chapter 1.

guests, a secular historian named Thomas Holland, explained how he had come to regard his view of the irrelevancy of the Church as wrong-headed. Holland's specialty is late antiquity, particularly the Romans and the Greeks. As he dug into Cicero, he began to recognize that Cicero's Roman world was truly alien to him. He reflected on the fact that Julius Caesar had killed a million Gauls and enslaved a million more all to advance his political career, and that Cicero did not regard this as evil in any way. He saw the same alien character in the Greeks and in early Islam—they accepted things as normal that any modern person would reject as horribly evil. And he began to realize that virtually all the things that explain modern sensibilities could be found, not in the Roman Empire, nor in the Greek philosophers, nor anywhere else in antiquity, but in Saint Paul's small set of letters. There, he found the backbone of Western morality and expectations. He wrote about this discovery of his in the British political journal *The New Statesman* in 2016. In his article he concluded,

> Today, even as belief in God fades across the West, the countries that were once collectively known as Christendom continue to bear the stamp of the two-millennia-old revolution that Christianity represents. It is the principal reason why, by and large, most of us who live in post-Christian societies still take for granted that it is nobler to suffer than to inflict suffering. It is why we generally assume that every human life is of equal value. In my morals and ethics, I have learned to accept that I am not Greek or Roman at all, but thoroughly and proudly Christian.[48]

In the *Unbelievable?* interview, Holland described how he sees that Paul's letters, along with the four gospel accounts, are the

---

[48] Holland, Tom, "Why I Was Wrong About Christianity," *New Statesman,* 14 September 2016, https://www.newstatesman.com/politics/religion/2016/09/tom-holland-why-i-was-wrong-about-christianity

most impactful writing to have emerged from the ancient world. He observed,

> If we're talking of Paul, I think of him as a kind of depth charge deep beneath the foundations of the classical world. It's not anything that you particularly notice if you're at Corinth or Alexandria. And then you start feeling this kind of rippling outwards. And by the time you get to the 11th century in Latin Christendom, everything has changed. Essentially ... he sets up ripple effects of revolution throughout Western history. So the 11th century where the papal revolution essentially establishes this idea that society has to be reborn, reconfigured, that vested interests have to be torn down... And then what we call the Reformation is a further ripple effect of that, and the Enlightenment is a further ripple effect of that. It's spilled out so much that now, in the 21st century, we don't even realize where these ripple effects are coming from. We just take them for granted.[49]

The modern world, with its sense of the worth of ordinary people, its recognition of God-given rights, its laws against slavery, rape, and child labor, its aim of universal literacy and political suffrage, not to mention its plentiful food, its inexpensive, machine-made clothing, its flush toilets and its aspirin tablets, is a vastly better place for billions of people than was the ancient world—and it's vastly better because of the persistent instruction of the Church.

Another convincing data point appeared in 2012 in the *American Political Science Review* in a peer-reviewed and widely accepted article written by Robert Woodberry.[50] Woodberry revolutionized

---

[49] https://www.youtube.com/watch?v=AIJ9gK47Ogw. The entire hour-long interview is available at https://www.youtube.com/watch?v=nlf_ULB26cU.

[50] Robert Woodberry, "The Missional Roots of Liberal Democracy," *American Political Science Review,* Vol. 106, No. 2, May 2012. One can download the published article from https://www.academia.edu/2128659/The_Missionary_Roots_of_Liberal_Democracy.

political science by connecting the rise of liberal democracies in the third world with the presence of what he called "conversionary Protestants" in the previous century. The presence of such missionaries turned out, in his fourteen years of research, to be a far more powerful predictor of where liberal democracy occurs than any variables previously considered— climate, health, location, accessibility, natural resources, colonial power, disease prevalence, and so forth. Woodberry noted,

> In particular, conversionary Protestants (CPs) were a crucial catalyst initiating the development and spread of religious liberty, mass education, mass printing, newspapers, voluntary organizations, most major colonial reforms, and the codification of legal protections for nonwhites in the nineteenth and early twentieth centuries. These innovations fostered conditions that made stable representative democracy more likely—regardless of whether many people converted to Protestantism. Moreover, religious beliefs motivated most of these transformations."[51]

Contemporary researchers had been more likely to assert that missionaries helped colonialists exploit third world cultures for their resources. There were colonial influences in many cases, but in fact conversional Protestants usually opposed such exploitation, exposing it in front of their congregations back home and bringing political pressure to bear to end it.[52]

The world continues to become a better place for more people as we go along. In 1981, according to the World Bank, 42% of the people of the world lived in extreme poverty, which they defined as having to subsist on the equivalent of $1.90 per day or less. By 2013 that number had fallen by a billion people, while the number of not-so-extremely-poor people on the planet had

---

[51] Ibid., pp. 244-245.

[52] Andrea Palpant Dilley, "The Surprising Discovery About Those Colonialist, Proselytizing Missionaries," *Christianity Today,* Jan/Feb 2014. Available at https://www.disciplenations.org/article/pdf-surprising-discovery-colonialist-proselytizing-missionaries/.

increased by four billion. The percentage of the world's population living in extreme poverty in 2013 was just shy of 11%, and the World Bank estimates that by 2016 it was closer to 9%.[53]

Could it be that the prophetic images from the Hebrew prophets have been fulfilled in part by the rise of Christianity in the West? Could the picture in Isaiah 60 of the Gentiles bringing their wealth and laying it at the Jews' feet have been partly fulfilled by the growing wealth of the Church in Europe? Might the picture of the nations saying "Let's go up to the house of the Lord so that He may teach us His ways" have been fulfilled already by the spread of liberty, human rights, and universal literacy from Western, Protestant nations to the rest of the world? Do billions of people now enjoy plentiful food, inexpensive clothing, warm houses in the winter and liberty to pursue their callings and desires because God has already begun to create the new earth that He promised? Might it have been the modern world that the Hebrew prophets foresaw?

I've never heard anybody defend that notion, but I suspect that it's closer to the truth than we dare to imagine. No, we have not created heaven on earth yet, but then, the game is not over. We might not have reached the third quarter, even. We can't know until it's over. But it appears to be the case that through the agency of the Messiah and His Church, God has begun lifting us, His lost and wandering charges, out of our poverty and ignorance and has gradually been making our lives better. And perhaps it will continue until the kingdom of heaven has leavened the entire lump of dough.

Though the disciples could not have foreseen the whole fulfillment of it, this was all implied when Jesus repeated the

---

[53] "The world has made great progress in eradicating extreme poverty," *The Economist*, March 30, 2017, https://www.economist.com/international/2017/03/30/the-world-has-made-great-progress-in-eradicating-extreme-poverty.

phrase, "theirs is the kingdom of heaven," to signal the topic of His sermon.

# Chapter 5: Modeling the Eternal Law

## Outline of the Sermon on the Mount
### Subject: Life in the Kingdom of God

| | | |
|---|---|---|
| I. God wants you to model His character... | | Matthew 5 |
| A. Ordinary believers are holy | | (5:3-12) |
| B. Your job is to demonstrate God's character | | (5:13-16) |
| C. The scriptures are your guide | | (5:17-20) |
| D. God's character is your standard | | |
| | 1. Hold relationships in highest esteem | (5:21-26) |
| | 2. Keep your desires ordinate | (5:27-30) |
| | 3. Speak truth at all times | (5:31-37) |
| | 4. Do good to all, not evil | (5:38-48) |
| | | |
| II. ...so give Him your whole-hearted devotion... | | Matthew 6-7:2 |
| A. Serve God, not reputation | | (6:1-18) |
| B. Serve God, not wealth | | (6:19-24) |
| C. Serve God, not self | | (6:25-7:2) |
| | | |
| III. ...and He will produce His character in you. | | Matthew 7:3-27 |
| A. Stay humble | | (7:3-6) |
| B. Pray for God's help | | (7:7-12) |
| C. Be diligent | | (7:13-14) |
| D. Stick to the Master's training | | (7:15-23) |
| E. He will make you unshakable | | (7:24-27) |

So Jesus announced that what He was about to say was about the kingdom of God. Having set up the topic, He proceeded to tell them that they, His *talmidim*, were to be included in the kingdom, and that their job was to model God's character for all those who were not so lucky as they. God's character, He assured them, was revealed in the scriptures and was reflected in His laws.

## Beatitudes

> Blessed are the poor in spirit, for theirs is the kingdom of
>     heaven.
> Blessed are those who mourn, for they shall be comforted.
> Blessed are the meek, for they shall inherit the earth.
> Blessed are those who hunger and thirst for righteousness, for
>     they shall be satisfied.
> Blessed are the merciful, for they shall receive mercy.
> Blessed are the pure in heart, for they shall see God.
> Blessed are the peacemakers, for they shall be called sons of
>     God.
> Blessed are those who are persecuted for righteousness' sake,
>     for theirs is the kingdom of heaven.
> Blessed are you when others revile you and persecute you and
>     utter all kinds of evil against you falsely on my account.
>     Rejoice and be glad, for your reward is great in heaven, for
>     so they persecuted the prophets who were before you.[1]

I began explaining, way back in chapter one, how the Beatitudes
were ordinary, Jewish prayers, *b'rakhas*, but with a funny twist.
The twist was that whereas ordinary *b'rakhas* bless God, when
Jesus offered His *b'rakhas* He was blessing His *talmidim*. His
point was to associate his students with God, the Almighty, and
by doing so to give them the task of representing Him clearly to
anybody who needed to see Him—which is ultimately
everybody, but especially those who actually want to see Him.

While I was preparing to write the first chapter of this book, I
googled "Beatitudes" and read the first six or seven articles that
the search engine returned. They were all pretty much the same,
and all painfully unhelpful; they had little of use to the Christian
life. The authors all mentioned the structure of the Beatitudes, a
list of paired conditions and results, but none of them offered
even a guess at why Jesus used that structure. A couple of them
confidently shuffled their meaning into the hereafter, since that

---

[1] Matthew 5:3-12

was their understanding of "the kingdom of heaven." Then all these articles launched into analyzing how each of the conditions Jesus listed would produce the associated result, as though Jesus were saying that there was something specific about being poor in spirit that would net them entrance into the kingdom of heaven, and so on.

I'm not going to say that there's zero connection between the listed conditions and their associated results in the Beatitudes. Because those pairs came out of His mouth that way, it seems reasonable to think that Jesus had those things associated somehow in His mind. It's likely that if we look for a connection between each condition and its supposed outcome, we'll find one. But I'm convinced that that was not the point that Jesus was trying to make and that if we focus on that we'll miss His point.

His point, rather, was to inform His students that they were welcome in God's holy kingdom, where all needs are met by God's favor, and that they were welcome just as they were. He was introducing them to the notion that because they were holy and blessed in that manner they had a job to do, namely to extend that favor to everybody else.

Jesus' entire ministry—birth, life, death, resurrection—can be described as a ministry of reconciliation; it was His job to reconcile Man to God. Man had become estranged from his Creator, and God's intent in Christ was to draw Man close to Himself again—hence all the prophetic talk of God walking among His people. Christian theology tells us that He accomplished this by His atoning death on the cross; and corresponding to that, a number of Jesus' sayings predict that sacrifice and its effect, like this one from John's gospel:

> Now is the judgment of this world; now will the ruler of this world be cast out. And I, when I am lifted up from the earth, will draw all people to myself."[2]

---

[2] John 12:31-32

But in addition to his dying, Jesus also drew them close to God through His teaching. His instruction in the gospels was not just filler to mark the time between His incarnation and His resurrection. Nor was it merely incidental, a side consequence of the many things He did that spoke of His divinity and authenticity. What Jesus taught was the basic instruction for the new kingdom that He was establishing, in which He Himself would be crowned king because of His obedience that led Him to the cross.[3]

In some of Jesus' sayings, reconciliation between God and Man took the form of His bringing God down to seem like one of us. This goes on, for example, in the places where Jesus compared God to a human father:

> ...which one of you, if his son asks him for bread, will give
> him a stone? Or if he asks for a fish, will give him a serpent?
> If you then, who are evil, know how to give good gifts to
> your children, how much more will your Father who is in
> heaven give good things to those who ask him![4]

The Beatitudes are an instance of Jesus going the other direction, elevating His disciples to make them seem holy like God Himself. The disciples were used to blessing God for His goodness and holiness: Jewish prayers are all about how great God is. By blessing His disciples using the same language, Jesus was emphasizing to them that they were of the same nature as God.

It was not the holiest among the disciples that Jesus identified with God. It was all of them, manifesting all the qualities of ordinary students. They were poor in spirit, meek, mourning, and hungering to be more righteous than they were. Some of them were even being reviled by other Jews. When Jesus blessed them

---

[3] NT Wright makes this point at length and persuasively in his book *How God Became King: the Forgotten Story of the Gospels*, op. cit.

[4] Matthew 7:8-11

the way Jews bless God, His point was that they didn't have to wait or achieve anything to be God's representatives; they already were, even if they were poor in spirit and meek in attitude.

All the results He described were things that anybody familiar with the Hebrew prophets would have recognized as things to be granted "on that day," the day on which the prophecies were to be fulfilled. Jesus was telling them that the kingdom of God was right at the door, and that they were all going to get the benefits of living in it: comfort for their sorrows, inheritance, dominion, righteousness, mercy, and privilege to see the face of God and to become sons of God. He wasn't saying that specific conditions would produce specific results, He was saying that every righteous desire would be fulfilled in the kingdom of God. His point was "If you're here and you're part of what I'm doing, the kingdom of heaven is yours, and you'll get what everybody gets in the kingdom of heaven."

But for God's representatives there was to be a cost. He ended the Beatitudes by comparing them to the prophets. They were like the prophets, first, in that they would receive great reward. Descriptions of heaven that one reads in Western Christendom don't usually mention that there will be differing levels of rank or recognition in heaven, but a large proportion of Jesus' statements about it make that point. He spoke often about how great or small one's reward will be.[5] And of course, since the kingdom of heaven was arriving any day, He was not just talking about what they would get at the end of the age but also where they might stand in the community that He was planting. That's why Paul, the Apostle, spoke of high status as his goal, and spoke of both present and future attainment: "I press on toward the goal for the prize of the upward call of God in Christ Jesus."[6]

---

[5] In addition to Matthew 5:12 and its parallel in Luke's gospel (Luke 6:23), see Matthew 10:41, Mark 9:41, Matthew 5:19, Matthew 5:46, and the beginning section of Matthew 6 where he mentions rewards seven times.

[6] Philippians 3:14

They were also like the prophets in that their role was similar: to represent God directly. And they were also like the prophets in that they were not going to get all that kingdom goodness for free; it was going to cost them what it had cost the prophets before them. They would be misunderstood, falsely accused, and reviled by those who did not appreciate what they were.

But what were they?

## Salt and Light

> You are the salt of the earth, but if salt has lost its taste, how shall its saltiness be restored? It is no longer good for anything except to be thrown out and trampled under people's feet.
>
> You are the light of the world. A city set on a hill cannot be hidden. Nor do people light a lamp and put it under a basket, but on a stand, and it gives light to all in the house. In the same way, let your light shine before others, so that they may see your good works and give glory to your Father who is in heaven.[7]

What they were to be was a clear picture of who God is. Their job was to reflect His nature.

This is hardly something new for anybody familiar with the sweep of Bible history. Man had existed in the presence of God, and had borne His image; but Man had fallen and chosen to follow lesser spirits,[8] sacrificing to them and worshiping them. God apportioned the nations to live under the dominion of those spirits,[9] but chose a nation for Himself through whom He

---

[7] Matthew 5:13-16

[8] See I Corinthians 10:19-20 and Deuteronomy 32:16-17. The idols were images of earthly things but represented worship of the demons, which are spirits.

intended to reveal His own nature and thus rescue mankind from the error into which it had fallen. That nation, the family of Abraham, had likewise failed in its task to represent His character properly, so He had chosen to do the job Himself through His special redeemer, the Messiah.

Now the Messiah was there, and His first order of business was to train students to do what Israel had been meant to do all along: represent God accurately. Jesus was never supposed to be one of a kind; believers are told that He was to be the first of many brothers who were to be just like Him.[10] So…Beatitudes. "You're holy, like God," followed by:

You are the salt of the earth…You are the light of the world.[11]

It's your job, said the Rabbi to His students, to preserve, season, and cauterize, to be seen, and to illuminate. It's your job to show the nations what their God truly is like.

While giving His students this picture of whom they were supposed to be by comparing them to salt, Jesus was also describing the state of the Hebrew nation. The nation was salt that had lost its flavor and was about to be trampled underfoot by men. He echoed this same idea during His last week as He wept over the nation's apostasy, reported in Matthew 23:37 and Luke 19:41. Jesus was prophesying over the nation, and warning His students that it was possible for them to fail horribly as well.

The city set on a hill would have been taken by Jesus' audience as a reference to Jerusalem. Jerusalem does sit on top of a cliff and cannot be hidden; but Jerusalem is also spoken of by the prophets as being elevated by God, as we saw in chapter four. Corresponding to these things, all references in the scriptures that speak of going to Jerusalem speak of it as going "up," and those

---

[9] See Heiser, op. cit., chapter 14.

[10] Romans 8:29

[11] Matthew 5:13a, 14a

that speak of going from Jerusalem to someplace else speak of it as going "down."

The lamps that were lit to be seen were in the temple, and also represented the Jewish nation. This usage of "lamp" to denote a representative of God's presence gets repeated at the beginning of John's Apocalypse as candlesticks representing the churches of Asia Minor.[12]

So as Jesus impressed upon His students their role as representatives of God, He reminded them of Israel's similar role and of the seriousness of Israel's failure to carry out that role.

I have already discussed Jesus' insistence that He came to establish "the Law [and] the Prophets." Emphasizing His orthodoxy at this point served to assure His students that accepting their exalted status as true representatives of God's character would not offend the Almighty, but was in fact what He had intended for them all along.

The rest of Matthew's fifth chapter consists of a series of six observations by Jesus about what His disciples may have heard from other teachers, followed by a description of how He wanted them to view those things instead. It's time now to take a look at those.

---

[12] Revelation 1:12

# Chapter 6: Rabbi Jesus Adjusts *Halakha*

## Outline of the Sermon on the Mount
### Subject: Life in the Kingdom of God

| | |
|---|---|
| I. God wants you to model His character... | Matthew 5 |
|    A. Ordinary believers are holy | (5:3-12) |
|    B. Your job is to demonstrate God's character | (5:13-16) |
|    C. The scriptures are your guide | (5:17-20) |
|    **D. God's character is your standard** | |
|       **1. Hold relationships in highest esteem** | **(5:21-26)** |
|       **2. Keep your desires ordinate** | **(5:27-30)** |
|       **3. Speak truth at all times** | **(5:31-37)** |
|       **4. Do good to all, not evil** | **(5:38-48)** |
| | |
| II. ...so give Him your whole-hearted devotion... | Matthew 6-7:2 |
|    A. Serve God, not reputation | (6:1-18) |
|    B. Serve God, not wealth | (6:19-24) |
|    C. Serve God, not self | (6:25-7:2) |
| | |
| III. ...and He will produce His character in you. | Matthew 7:3-27 |
|    A. Stay humble | (7:3-6) |
|    B. Pray for God's help | (7:7-12) |
|    C. Be diligent | (7:13-14) |
|    D. Stick to the Master's training | (7:15-23) |
|    E. He will make you unshakable | (7:24-27) |

Many interpreters take the last part of Matthew 5 to be Jesus' repudiation of the Jewish law as it was taught in those days. That's what I thought, too, when I was younger. It turns out that that's not at all what it was.

## S'mikhah

Rather, it was the ordinary teaching style of a Rabbi who possessed what Jews would call s'mikhah. The word means roughly "authority," and later on it was used to indicate formal ordination. Literally the word means "to lean" and refers to how the Rabbis would lay hands on a candidate to confer authority on him, intending to convey the spirit of the older Rabbi onto the new Rabbi. The practice began with Moses laying his hands, first on seventy elders to give them authority to interpret law for the Israelites,[1] and then on Joshua as his successor.[2] In Jesus' day they believed that there existed an unbroken chain of authority back to Moses, who was the first and greatest Rabbi.[3]

S'mikhah was usually transmitted by a court of three leaders, only one of whom needed to possess s'mikhah himself.[4] It could also be conferred by a lone Rabbi with s'mikhah onto one of his students if circumstances required it.[5]

One was not usually called "Rabbi" who did not possess s'mikhah. The Jews of that period would call local teachers "Rav," a similar word that could mean more or less what we mean today when call somebody "sir." Relevant to our topic here, men called "Rav" could teach Torah but had no authority to interpret. They could teach what the community understood to be true of the Torah and they could quote the great Rabbis on each of the topics, but they could not add their own opinions or interpretations.

---

[1] Numbers 11:16-25

[2] Numbers 27:15-23, Deuteronomy 34:9

[3] The chain of authority was broken during the Middle Ages. Modern Rabbis do receive ordination, but it is no longer necessarily connected to the original authority from Moses.

[4] Talmud, Tractate Sanhedrin 13b

[5] Talmud, Tractate Sanhedrin 14a

Once a Rabbi had been recognized and elevated by other Rabbis with *s'mikhah*, he was entitled to interpret. From then on, his teaching could take the form, "You've heard *this*, but I say to you that it means *that*." The authority to interpret gave these Rabbis the power to make *halakhic* decisions, decisions in Jewish law,[6] consistent with the seventy elders whom Moses commissioned to judge among the Israelites. As a Rabbi with *s'mikhah* teaching disciples, Jesus would have been expected to convey His interpretations of various points of *halakha*; if He had not had *s'mikhah*, it would have been improper for Him to do so.

Rabbis traveled a long road to obtain *s'mikhah*. The *Talmud* says that men are ready to teach at thirty, but that's not the same as interpreting. The great Rabbis of the *Talmud* were much older than that when they received *s'mikhah*: Rabbi Akiva was sixty, Rabbi Hillel was seventy, and Rabbi Shammai was eighty five.[7] It was an unheard-of thing for a young man like Jesus to be able to teach with authority.

The oddness of a Rabbi having *s'mikhah* at the age of thirty is one of the reasons why Matthew's gospel notes, after the Sermon on the Mount, that the people were amazed at His teaching.[8] It wasn't just the excellence of the content, although that was likely part of their reaction. Nor was it just that He was not giving them complex and confusing rules like those in the *Mishna*, although that's also likely part of their reaction, as I explained back in chapter three. The fact that He could teach His own interpretation at all was remarkable since He was so young. "Teaching them as one who had authority" is almost certainly referring to *s'mikhah*, and "not as their scribes" likely refers to Torah teachers who were not permitted to interpret.

---

[6] *Talmud*, Tractate *Sanhedrin* 5b

[7] Vander Laan, op. cit. The ages at which the sages received their authority appears to be the subject of tradition and may even appear in the Talmud, but I'm not sure where.

[8] Matthew 7:28-29

The question of *s'mikhah* was important because it spoke to them about what they could expect from the Rabbi. That's why we see so many instances in the gospels of teachers asking Jesus where He got authority to teach. They wanted to know what school of thought He represented and who had taught Him. It was not disrespectful of the leaders to ask, it was expected, though some of those conversations in the gospels clearly were hostile.

A lot of Jewish culture, both then and now, rests on intense, passionate wrestling with the ideas in the Law, attempting to arrive at the truth. Loud arguments were the norm, not the exception, and would not have been considered breaches of social order the way they are in the Gentile West. When we see the description "they tested Jesus,"[9] we should not take it as some underhanded attempt to trip Him up, except in those passages where the writer specifically says that that was the goal. "Testing" was how the Rabbis and their students communicated with each other, and how they learned and grew.

The body of teaching that distinguished an authoritative Rabbi's interpretation from that of other Rabbis would be referred to as his "yoke." This is what Jesus was talking about when, in Matthew 11, He invited those who were burdened to come to Him to find rest for their souls; "My yoke is easy" was an assurance that His take on *halakha* was in some way easier to bear than what they might learn from other Rabbis.[10] It would rest more easily on their souls.

We may actually have some information about Jesus' *s'mikhah*.[11] Beginning at Luke 20:1, during the last week of His life, some members of the Sanhedrin approached Him and asked where He had received *s'mikhah*. Now, the manner of good Rabbis when challenged was to answer the question that had been put to them with another question, as an invitation to examine the matter in

---

[9] See, for instance, Matthew 16:1, Matthew 19:3, or Matthew 22:35.

[10] Matthew 11:28-30

[11] Vander Laan, op. cit.

greater depth. The Rabbi's question would contain the answer, or at least a pointer to the answer, to the original question. So when Jesus responded in the manner of the Rabbis, "Let me ask you a question: was the baptism of John from God, or from men?" He was probably implying that John the Baptist had conferred *s'mikhah* on Him when he baptized Him. According to the text, the leaders declined to answer His question because they did not want to acknowledge John's authority but were afraid of the reaction of onlookers if they didn't. Consistent with the pattern of Rabbinic teaching, when they refused to answer the question Jesus ended the conversation.

We do know that Jesus had received His ministry when He was baptized by John, and that John already knew Him at that time.[12] But we also know that Jesus received approval directly from God at that time: "You are My beloved son, in whom I am well-pleased."[13] So in fact, Jesus may have received *s'mikhah* from two sources: from John, and from God, the Father. He may have been confirming this in John 5:31-36 when He said that those testifying to His authority were John, the Baptist, and God, the Father.

While *s'mikhah* was usually conferred by a court of three judges, it could also be conferred by a Rabbi with *s'mikhah* on one of his students,[14] so *s'mikhah* directly from John would have been valid if John had *s'mikhah* himself and if Jesus had been one of his students at some point during his youth.

And of course, if God, the Almighty, pronounces that one has authority to speak on His behalf, who can tell Him otherwise? Jesus was the only Rabbi in history to receive *s'mikhah* directly from God. When I get to talking about the *Khasidim* in chapter eight, we'll see that the Jews recognized that God sometimes bends the rules for special cases.

---

[12] Implied by the exchange in Matthew 3:13-15.

[13] Luke 3:21-22

[14] *Talmud*, Tractate *Sanhedrin* 14a

The point here is that the six comparisons in Matthew 5 between what the disciples had heard and what Jesus wanted them to learn instead were the expected pattern of instruction from a Rabbi with *halakhic* authority. It implied no general disapproval of *halakha* or of Jewish teaching in general. In fact, the pattern rested on the authority conferred by *halakha*, and the discussion was the sort of adjustment of *halakha* in which authoritative Rabbis engaged all the time.[15]

## What Was Original About Jesus' Instruction

Having begun by announcing to His students that their job was to reflect accurately the character of their Father, Jesus proceeded to adjust *halakha* in such a way as to bring it into conformity with the true Law of God. He did not have to change everything in Jewish Law in order to accomplish that; mostly it was a matter of refocusing and showing His students which parts to emphasize and which to ignore.

A lot of Jesus' instruction was repetition of ethics taught by the Rabbis of His day. For instance, there was no disagreement among Jews that the *Shema* was the greatest commandment of the Law.[16] While not all Jews would have agreed that "love your neighbor as yourself" was the second greatest, the House of Hillel did teach that. (I'll say more about this in the next chapter.) Hillel also famously taught that the entire Law was expressed by

---

[15] A similar point was made by Viljoen, Francois, in "Jesus' halakhic argumentation on the true intent of the law," *Verbum et Ecclesia*, (Online) vol. 30, no. 1, Praeetoria, Jan 2013. Available at http://www.scielo.org.za/scielo.php?script=sci_arttext&pid=S2074-77052013000100009.

[16] The *Shema* begins, "Hear, O Israel! The LORD is our God, the LORD alone!" and proceeds "You shall love the LORD your God with all your heart, all your soul, and all your strength..." The full prayer appears in Deuteronomy 6:4-9. In Matthew 22:36-40 and similar passages Jesus quoted an abbreviated version, but every Jew hearing Him would automatically have assumed that He meant the entire prayer.

"What is hateful to you, do not to your neighbor," observing that the rest of the Law was just commentary on that central precept, much like Jesus said in Matthew 22:37-40.[17] Jesus ben Sirach, writing at about 185 BCE, said "Pardon your neighbor any wrongs done to you, and when you pray, your sins will be forgiven,"[18] which is similar to what Jesus taught in Matthew 6:14-15. Jesus' instruction concerning saving animals on the Sabbath[19] was based on common *midrash*, as were a number of Jesus' parables. So a great deal of what Jesus taught was already present in the words of the Rabbis.

David Flusser, a Jewish Professor of New Testament at Hebrew University, observed

> From ancient Jewish writings we could easily construct a whole Gospel without using a single word that originated with Jesus. This could only be done, however, because we do in fact possess the Gospels.[20]

Flusser makes the point here that while few if any individual points of Jesus' instruction may have been original, the sum of His collection and presentation of the Law were unique to Him. There was plenty of wisdom embedded within *halakhic* teaching; Jesus identified the wheat and discarded the chaff.

We have already seen how Rabbi Jesus acknowledged a higher law from God to which *halakha* was supposed to point but sometimes didn't (or to which it pointed imperfectly), a way of living to which all the Jewish scriptures testified. And we have seen also how, regardless of the piety of certain individuals in Judaism, Jesus called the nation salt that had lost its flavor. Jesus

---

[17] *Talmud*, Tractate *Shabbat* 31a. Versions of the Golden Rule show up in lots of pre-Christian writing; I list several in chapter nine.

[18] Ecclesiasticus 28:2

[19] Luke 13:15, Luke 14:5

[20] Flusser, David, *Jesus*, The Hebrew University Press, Jerusalem, 1997, third edition, p.90.

used His *halakhic* authority to steer His disciples toward conduct that would represent God's character more accurately; that was His goal. So we can take His versions of the Law as representing patterns of conduct that God had intended from the beginning—patterns that His *talmidim* were to take to others. That's why He sums up His discussion of *halakha*,

> "You therefore must be perfect, as your heavenly Father is perfect."[21]

The statement summarizes the entire sermon up to that point, the whole of Matthew's fifth chapter. Jesus' object was conduct that accurately reflected the character of God, the Almighty.

## A Better Fence Around the Law

Rabbinic teachers attempted to "build a fence around the law,"[22] as I mentioned back in chapter three. Some Rabbis on certain topics asserted that they could not be certain exactly what it was that offended God, and their fence around the law was intended to prevent people from even getting close to offending. For instances from more modern Judaism, where the law said "You shall not boil the meat of a kid in the milk of its mother,"[23] the Rabbis forbade not just boiling but eating milk products and meat at the same meal or serving them on the same dishes. Another instance occurred when Rabbinic tradition advised Jews to avoid saying the name of God or even mentioning the word "God," reasoning that if they never said God's name they would never take it in vain.

---

[21] Matthew 5:48

[22] *Talmud*, Tractate *Avot* 1.1. "Moshe received the Torah from Sinai and transmitted it to Yehoshua, and Yehoshua to the Elders, and the Elders to the Prophets, and the Prophets transmitted it to the Men of the Great Assembly. They said three things: Be deliberate in judgment, raise up many disciples and make a fence for the Torah."

[23] Exodus 23:19, Exodus 34:26, Deuteronomy 14:21

Closer to Jesus' time, the *Mishna* contains a third instance, criticizing the sort of *P'rushim* (Pharisees) that they called "blood-letting *P'rushim*." These were overly pious men who avoided lusting by shutting or lowering their eyes when they approached a woman, with the result that they sometimes walked into things and bruised their foreheads. The Rabbis of the *Mishna* regarded this behavior to be foolish.[24]

Jesus built the fence along a more practical line. Where some of the other teachers counseled avoiding entire issues in order to be safe, Jesus focused on the specific attitudes of the heart that could lead to bigger sins.[25] He observed that one could best avoid great sins like adultery and murder by addressing the smaller, more ordinary habits of thought that would eventually lead to them. His approach was to temper one's inner thoughts to reflect the Law of God before one ever encountered a situation where a greater sin was possible. "Don't allow lust to dwell and you will never fall into adultery. Don't stew in your hate for your brother, and you'll never be tempted to murder him. Develop the habit of saying what you mean, and you'll never need to make an oath, let alone risk breaking one."[26]

Jesus was addressing a truth about great sins: people don't just hop into them, they build up to them over time.[27] Great sin is the

---

[24] *Talmud*, Tractate *Sotah* 22b. Notice that Jesus was not the only Jew to criticize this approach to holiness; the *Gemara* at this point treats the blood-letting Pharisees, along with several other types, as pseudo-righteous. It is possible that the seven woes that Jesus pronounced on "scribes and Pharisees, hypocrites" in Matthew 23:13-33 parallel the seven types of pseudo-righteous discussed in *Sotah* 22b. See http://www.fishingtheabyss.com/archives/116 for an analysis attempting to establish this.

[25] As we'll see in a moment, though, Jesus addressed the entire issue of oaths by saying "Just don't make them." This differs from the approach of the "bloody *P'rushim*" in that what Jesus was advising, simply speaking the truth, was always the righteous thing to do, whereas shutting one's eyes when approaching a woman was fairly ridiculous.

[26] There is a similar discussion of Jesus' approach in Flusser, *Jesus*, op. cit., pp. 90-91.

result of a way of life, a pattern of conduct given over to a character flaw. The Apostle James described this process: "…each person is tempted when he is lured and enticed by his own desire. Then desire when it has conceived gives birth to sin, and sin when it is fully grown brings forth death."[28] The phrases "when it has conceived" and "when it is fully grown" point to a process that takes time, possibly a great deal of time. Jesus would have agreed.

The Amorites mentioned in Genesis 15 illustrate this process. In Genesis 15 we hear God explaining to Abram the future of his family, how they would migrate elsewhere and be enslaved for four generations, then would return to possess the land where he was standing. His explanation was, "…for the iniquity of the Amorites is not yet complete."[29] God implied that He was going to judge the Amorites for their sins by removing them from the land and giving the land to Abram's descendants; only, the full measure of sins that would justify that judgment had not all been committed yet, from the human, time-bound point of view. God, working within our universe's time, would not remove them before they had earned that removal. The sin that would justify that judgment had already been born, so to speak, but it was not fully grown. God standing outside of time, however, saw that the outcome of the process was inevitable. God told Abram that once the Amorites' sins had produced what they were going to produce (four generations later), they would be judged and annihilated, and the judgment would be just at that time.

Jesus' general approach to sins, illustrated in His discussion of *halakha*, addressed that process in practical fashion by advising, "Don't start down that road and you'll never reach that destination." Form good habits of conduct in the first place based

---

[27] One of my favorite modern aphorisms, from William F. Buckley, makes the same observation: "I profoundly believe it takes a lot of practice to become a moral slob."

[28] James 1:14-15

[29] Genesis 15:13-16, especially verse 16.

on proper attitudes, counseled Jesus, and one will never fall into serious trouble.

Of course, Jesus' object was not merely that His students avoid the greater sins. A community in which all the participants deal with their animosities while they're still fresh is a healthy, friendly community from which everybody benefits (although it may feature more low-level confrontations than we might otherwise be used to). Likewise, everybody benefits in a community in which people divert their sensual desires in better directions before they become obsessions or vile acts. Part of Jesus' point, in each of His *halakhic* discussions, was that behavior could become offensive to God, damaging to the community, and dangerous to their souls long before they crossed one of the bright, red boundaries. But the starting point for Jesus' instruction was the Law of Moses, and the Law specified the big sins. Jesus reasoned from there to an understanding of God's character and intent in which the community avoided great sin by addressing the seeds of sin while they were still small.

Jesus' commands were not laws so much as they were goals. He was explaining a set of attitudes that He intended would characterize life in the righteous kingdom that He was planting. He had already explained this in His introduction to His discussion of *halakha*, in Matthew 5:17-20. I pointed this out in chapter three, how that paragraph would have been heard as encouragement to discover the character of God in the scriptures because simply following *halakha* would not produce the sort of righteousness that God demanded. Jesus proceeded from that point to instruct His students to cultivate the attitudes of the heart that would lead to godly conduct, rather than telling them to adhere to scrupulous laws that forbade specific behaviors.

Jesus was not the only Rabbi to make this point about avoiding sin by dealing with its roots, but we can take Jesus' version to reflect accurately the higher Law of God.

## Offenses

Jesus began His discussion of *halakha* by claiming that interpersonal anger could actually be prosecuted as though a murder had been committed. We have to take this as hyperbole since the law was never adjusted to make bad attitudes prosecutable as He described, but it's hyperbole with a clear point. Jesus' object was to explain that ordinary dislikes between people constitute an offense against God in the kingdom of heaven and need to be addressed immediately as a top priority. Anger leads to hatred, and hatred eventually to murder; so His *talmidim* were to deal with anger before that progression got anywhere. Paul echoed this approach later in his letter to the Ephesians: "...do not let the sun go down on your anger, and give no opportunity to the devil."[30]

Jesus was making it plain that interpersonal hatred is not just offensive to God, it's costly to us. When He spoke in Matthew 5:25-26 of how one's adversary might prosecute the crime of hatred, He was describing what happens between people even when there's not a formal, legal charge. Once people become alienated, there's no recovery until the entire interpersonal debt gets paid. "A brother offended is more unyielding than a strong city, and quarreling is like the bars of a castle," says Proverbs 18:19. So the wise course is to settle disputes before people become truly offended, because once offended, they can hardly be won back. "Truly, I say to you, you will never get out until you have paid the last penny."[31]

Jesus used an illustration here the point of which we moderns tend to miss. He said this:

> So if you are offering your gift at the altar and there
> remember that your brother has something against you, leave

---

[30] Ephesians 4:26b
[31] Matthew 5:26

your gift there before the altar and go. First be reconciled to your brother, and then come and offer your gift.[32]

It's easy to see the direction of Jesus' instruction: staying on good terms with our fellow-citizens in the kingdom of God is more important than sacrifice or religious duty. Jesus made this point in several places in the gospels.[33]

The part that we might miss because we don't know His culture is how emphatic Jesus was being; He was using outrageous hyperbole. There was only one temple in Judaism. Jews traveled from all over the region to visit it three times a year, all at the same time. After a long trip on foot leading a large and expensive animal (or purchasing such an animal in Jerusalem), they might have had to wait in a long line of supplicants, possibly for a very long time, until a priest was available to sacrifice it. The travel, purchasing, and waiting, combined, might have taken a full week. Interrupting the process after one had finally reached the altar would have been ridiculous.

It would be like one of us in modern America having been invited to present a paper to the Secretary of the Interior, and once having traveled to Washington, been admitted to the Executive Office Building, shaken the Secretary's hand and been seated in his office, suddenly leaping up and telling the him, "Hold on; don't move; I really have to take care of this first," and then stepping out of the office to make a phone call to settle a dispute with your friend George. You wouldn't get back into the Secretary's office. The opportunity would have passed.

And what Jesus was saying was that interpersonal relationships were so much more important than religious observance that something so completely outrageous as getting all the way to the altar and then leaving one's place there would be reasonable if it would save a relationship.

---

[32] Matthew 5:23-24

[33] See, for example, Matthew 12:1-8 or Luke 10:25-37.

## Lust

Similarly, Jesus made the point that one can avoid adultery if one addresses lust before it gets to the point of acting on it. The observation that the one who lusts "has already committed adultery in his heart" was not aimed at creating guilt, nor was it a claim that God will punish the person who lusts inside himself with the same measure as one who actually commits adultery. Rather, it was a warning that the smaller sin, left to fester and grow, would lead to the larger sin, or to sins just as destructive.

Jesus advising His students to dismember themselves was hyperbole, of course, but it pointed out how important it was to address the problem. Lust is pleasant and fulfills a need; a person who cherishes his lusts can feel as though giving them up means losing a part of himself. Jesus acknowledged this but reasoned "better to lose a part of yourself than to lose your self entirely."

At the same time, His hyperbole forced the hearers to make an assessment about where the problem came from, avoiding the silliness of the blood-letting *P'rushim*. Tearing out eyes won't help anything at all, because the problem isn't with the eyes. Cutting off hands (or other parts) won't help, because the problem isn't with the hands. The problem is with the desires of the heart, and it is in the heart that harmful things we cherish need to be cut off.

## Divorce

Misunderstanding the issue that Jesus was addressing in Matthew 5:31-32 has caused a great deal of damage and pain in the Church.[34] To those unfamiliar with the history of Jewish law,

34 This topic is addressed in complete fashion in Instone-Brewer, David, *Divorce and Remarriage in the Church,* Intervarsity Press, Downer's Grove, IL, 2003. My brief discussion about divorce here is based mostly on Dr. Instone-Brewer's analysis.

Matthew 5:32 reads as though no cause for divorce is valid besides adultery, and also that remarriage after a divorce is simply forbidden. It turns out that that was not at all what Jesus intended. Still, He expressed God's desire for stable marriages and His general disapproval of divorce, and that's accurate.

The topic of divorce in the *Talmud* is huge; there are ninety separate sections in Tractate *Gittin*, the section of the *Talmud* dealing with the *git*, the certificate of divorce.[35] However, the teaching about divorce in the Torah is brief and is based on only two passages. The first passage is Exodus 21:7-11, which appears to deal with the case of a man who acquires a female slave and then takes her to his bed. In this passage, the Torah says that the woman is entitled to food, clothing, and sexual rights as his wife for as long as she lives. The sages reasoned that if the rights mentioned there were granted to a slave, how much more were they the rights of a free woman of Israel? Based on their reading of Exodus 21, the Rabbis said that a man was entitled to divorce his wife if she abused him physically or psychologically, abandoned him entirely, or refused him sexual access. In practice, they would grant the wife a divorce for similar reasons.[36]

The second passage is Deuteronomy 24:1, which says that if a man is engaged to be married and finds some cause of indecency in his fiancé, he may write her a certificate of divorce. This is the passage from which Jesus was speaking when He said that adultery was a valid cause for divorce.

---

[35] *Git* also refers to writs of manumission, which are documents declaring an indentured servant or slave to be free, and those are also discussed in Tractate *Gittin*. However, the bulk of the tractate is about divorce.

[36] Divorce rules in the *Talmud* are written so as to enable men to divorce their wives, not women to divorce their husbands. However, in practice the Rabbis granted similar protections to women. http://www.come-and-hear.com/gittin/index.html#intro. Though a woman could not hand her husband a *git*, the Rabbis could force a man to give his wife a *git* and accomplish the same thing. http://www.jewishencyclopedia.com/articles/5238-divorce.

There was a dispute in Jesus' day arising from an innovation in the interpretation of Deuteronomy 24:1 introduced by Rabbi Hillel, who was born about a hundred years before Jesus. According to Tractate *Gittin* 90 in the *Mishna*, the House of Hillel maintained that the phrase "a cause of indecency" or "a thing of unseemliness" actually mentioned two, separate things: indecency, and "a thing." They argued that because it said "a thing," a man could obtain a divorce for causes far less serious than indecency; they actually wrote that it was sufficient cause for divorce if she burned his dinner (Rabbis in the related *Gemara* added that she would have to have burned it on purpose). The House of Shammai disagreed, arguing that the passage only supported divorce in cases of indecency. It's worth noting that "indecency" was not just adultery, but could also be things like a woman flirting flagrantly in public with a man other than her husband.

The innovation that Hillel and his students introduced was called a "divorce for any cause." The practice actually gets mentioned in Matthew 19, where in verse 3 it says "Pharisees came up to [Jesus] and tested him by asking, 'Is it lawful to divorce one's wife for any cause?'" They were asking specifically about His position regarding Hillel's innovative reading of Deuteronomy 24:1. Jesus' answer also spoke specifically to that passage, and his language closely parallels the positions taken by the House of Shammai in the *Gemara* portions and *midrashim* that address this question.[37]

We see Hillel's innovation in use at the beginning of Matthew's gospel. The text reads as follows:

> When his mother Mary had been betrothed to Joseph, before they came together she was found to be with child from the

---

[37] *Sifre* Deuteronomy 269; Jerusalem *Talmud* Tractate *Sota* 1.2, 16b; Babylonian *Talmud* Tractate *Gittin* 9.10. Citations here were copied from Instone-Brewer, op. cit., chapter 5, note 3. "*Sifre*" refers to a collection of *halakhic midrashim*.

Holy Spirit. And her husband Joseph, being a just man and unwilling to put her to shame, resolved to divorce her quietly.[38]

"Divorce her quietly" in this case meant a divorce "for any cause," based on Hillel's interpretation. To obtain a divorce on other grounds would have required that Joseph prove to the local Rabbis that his betrothed, Mary, had been unfaithful. That would have been easy enough to do since she was pregnant and they had not had sex, but it would have permanently damaged her reputation and probably would have prevented her from marrying anyone else. However, obtaining a divorce "for any cause" would not require him to harm her reputation; he only had to say that she displeased him. She could have gone off for a few months and had the baby elsewhere, given him up for adoption, and then returned with her reputation intact. He used this law because he was "unwilling to put her to shame."

Not mentioned but probably also true is that Joseph would not have had to pay the *mohar* (bride-price) if he proved that his betrothed was unfaithful, but would likely have had to pay her a divorce penalty of two hundred shekels of silver if he divorced her "for any cause."[39] By protecting her reputation he would also have cost himself a fair amount of money. Fortunately for him, the Holy Spirit intervened and saved him the money.

In the view of the writer of Matthew's gospel (and me), all of this concern for Mary without concern for his own interests made Joseph "a just man."

At any rate, Jesus' claim that divorce was only permitted in instances of adultery was a response to Hillel's interpretation of Deuteronomy 24:1, and was not intended to change Jewish Law

---

[38] Matthew 1:18b-19

[39] Conditions for non-payment of *ketubot* (divorce penalty specified in the marriage contract) are discussed in *Talmud*, Tractate *Ketubot* 7. The topic of the *mohar* (bride-price) in ancient times up to Jesus' day is discussed at https://www.myjewishlearning.com/article/ancient-jewish-marriage/.

regarding anything arising from the other passage, Exodus 21. He was not saying that cruelty or abandonment were not legitimate grounds for divorce; He was merely saying that Deuteronomy 24:1 addressed adultery and not any other cause. This was also the clear point of His discussion of divorce law in Matthew 19.

But in general, Jesus taught that God stands opposed to divorce, and that divorces should only occur because of significant human failure.

## Oaths

Oaths and vows were apparently very common in Jesus' day. An entire tractate of the *Mishna*, Tractate *Nedarim*, is devoted to vows: defining terms, describing different ways of making vows, identifying which were valid and which were not, explaining how, when, and why vows could be broken, and so forth. Vows were made for all sorts of reasons; chapters of *Nedarim* cover business transactions, Nazirite vows, engagement vows, vows made in anger, etc.

When making oaths of abstinence from foods or activities, the common formula dictated the declaration, "Let so-and-so be to me as *korban*," which was a reference to a sacrifice in the Temple.[40] The culture was so temple-centered that they tried to link their strong intentions to the religious order. Jesus mentioned this practice in Mark 7:9-13, where He objected that their traditions created situations where people were forbidden by their own oaths from keeping obligations to their parents. In His view this violated God's true law.

In general, the Rabbis frowned on making vows. In *Nedarim* 9a, the *Mishna* observes that vows made "as the vow of the wicked"

---

[40] Freedman, Rabbi Dr. H., Introduction to the translation of Babylonian *Talmud*, Tractate *Nedarim*, http://www.come-and-hear.com/nedarim/index.html.

were valid in certain cases, but vows made "as the vow of the righteous" were not—apparently because they felt there was no such thing as a vow of the righteous. The *Gemara* in *Nedarim* 9a quoted Ecclesiastes, "It is better not to vow than to vow and not pay."[41] Rabbi Meir added, "Better than both is not to vow at all," but Rabbi Judah replied, "Better than both is to vow and repay."[42]

Jesus appears to have agreed with Rabbi Meir. To Him, all the complications of the subject could be avoided if one simply did as God advised and spoke plainly.

His list of things not to vow by is revealing. In Deuteronomy, the Almighty declared to the nation of Israel that they were to swear only by His name.[43] Here in Matthew, Jesus listed things that people apparently swore by that were anything but God's name: heaven, earth, Jerusalem, and their own heads. If we add Matthew 23:16-22, oaths were also made by the temple and the gold in the temple, and by the altar and the sacrifices on the altar. None of these were permissible under God's true law. We have to take Jesus' comments here as more than just a recommendation to speak plainly; He was also commanding complete devotion to the God of Israel by denouncing oaths made in reference to anything less than His holy name.

There's a connection between truth and devotion to God, of course. Oaths can be used as part of a self-important pretense, attempting to make ourselves sound more serious than we might without them. On the other hand, if we want to draw close to God, we must speak plainly and live in the truth. Those are opposites. Deception of any sort, even mildly self-important posturing, pushes us away from God. We have to drop all pretenses if we want to be His friends.

---

[41] Ecclesiastes 5:5

[42] Freedman, Rabbi Dr. H., op. cit.

[43] Deuteronomy 6:13, Deuteronomy 10:20

Paul, the Apostle, used oaths in no fewer than five of his letters—always calling God as his witness.[44] Either Jesus was not making law here against all oaths, or Paul sinned as a habit. I do not think that Jesus was forbidding oaths made in God's name as recommended in the Torah. Rather, I think that He was adjusting a habit of the culture, bringing it back in line with God's original intent. I think that Paul's use of oaths was in line with that intent.

## Do Not Resist the Evil Person

If we take Jesus' instruction not to resist "the evil person" as a law forbidding Christians from defending themselves, we create a law that makes Christians easy targets for every evil scheme. If we take it, on the other hand, as a strategy for dealing with individuals who manifest evil traits, it becomes useful and powerful.

I remember when I started seeing this principle in action. I happened across a video of Dr. Jordan Peterson discussing the first of his "Twelve Rules for Life," which is "Stand up straight with your shoulders back," or in some versions, "Stop being pathetic."[45] In this particular interview, Peterson explained that the crouched, bent-over position of a defeated, insecure person protects that person's soft parts, but that the upright position of the confident makes those soft parts vulnerable while at the same time announcing, "I can handle the vulnerability." He then mentioned what he called 'the Matthew principle," which is a quotation from Rabbi Jesus: "For to the one who has, more will be given, and he will have an abundance. But from the one who has not, even what he has will be taken away."[46] It's true:

---

[44] Romans 1:9, II Corinthians 1:23, Galatians 1:20, Philippians 1:8, I Thessalonians 2:5

[45] https://www.youtube.com/watch?v=Uq3Fh2eQ9Ls. The book is Peterson, Dr. Jordan, *Twelve Rules for Life: An Antidote to Chaos*, Luminate Psychological Services, Ltd., 2018.

[46] Matthew 13:12

confidence increases the likelihood of succeeding, while acting pathetic increases the likelihood of failing, in everything. Plus, whenever a person does something confidently and succeeds at it, that person increases the likelihood that they will succeed at the next thing they do as well.

Finally Peterson announced, "Isn't that the message of the Crucifixion? To accept the vulnerability of being?"

I remember feeling stunned and a little embarrassed that a secular psychologist grasped one of the central themes of the cross better than I did. Peterson was correct, though. Jesus announced it plainly. He did not have to die, He chose to. "Couldn't I ask my Father, and He'd send twelve legions of angels to rescue me?"[47] He became vulnerable by choice, out of His strength. He allowed Himself to be murdered in a most horrible fashion by evil men. By this He demonstrated the character of God, who does not have to allow such things but chooses to allow them so that He can rescue those who are murdering Him.

In this way Jesus forever buried the ancient world and replaced it with ours in which each individual can ennoble the lives of others who have less than they do: "For you were called to freedom, brothers. Only do not use your freedom as an opportunity for the flesh, but through love serve one another."[48]

Jesus was teaching this principle to His students. He was not making an absolute law that they were to obey in every instance; His object was to bring them to a place of personal holiness, confidence, and security in Him. From there they would have enough confidence to allow themselves to be vulnerable to wicked people, without the wickedness of those people actually harming their souls—not to become victims of cons or control games, but to call those playing those games to a more productive life.

---

[47] Matthew 26:53, my paraphrase.

[48] Galatians 5:13

I've seen godly men obey Jesus' instructions in instances where foolish people raise common but insulting errors about passages in scripture, for one example. They might say, "God broke His own commandment when He commanded the Israelites to commit genocide." My impulse is to dismiss such people as mockers with a comment like "You have a kindergartener's understanding of the Old Testament. Come back and discuss it after you've graduated high school." That would be rude, but it would also be addressing their evil directly, "eye for eye and tooth for tooth." My impulse illustrates what Jesus was saying not to do.

Wiser men say something like, "That's a good question. Let's examine it together," and break out a Bible to examine the passage. The wiser approach obeys Jesus' instruction; it gives the evil person what he's asking for and more. It takes the sting out of resisting their evil and makes it possible to approach them and win them.

I think that this is what Jesus was getting at. He was saying, "Don't automatically treat evil people as their evil deserves. Find a way to treat them as though they were your friends, and see whether they can be redeemed."

Later on we see Paul, the Apostle, preventing himself from being whipped by raising a legal point about punishing citizens of Rome.[49] A legalistic view of Matthew 5:38-42 might lead someone to tell Paul to let the centurion whip him twice, but I'm pretty sure that that's not what Jesus intended.

## Love Your Enemies

Jesus' discussion of loving one's enemies, the last point in Jesus' adjustments of *halakhah*, both wrapped up His exposition regarding how it was His disciples' job to represent God's

---

[49] Acts 22:25

character accurately, and introduced the next section of the Sermon on the Mount, His call to undivided devotion. I'm going to be discussing the model supplied in *Tanakh* for loving one's enemies in the next chapter. For now, I will simply observe how Jesus' adjustments to *halakha* all aimed at producing a friendlier world than that which the ancients were used to. The description of the fallen world supplied in Genesis 6 said that the earth was "corrupt" and "filled with violence." Jesus' instructions, like those of many of the Rabbis of His day, cut at the root of this corruption and violence, commending instead deliberate reconciliation, self-restraint, fidelity, honesty, patience, tolerance, and favor. On the basis of just this brief set of changes we might possibly be able to explain the entire difference between attitudes in the ancient world and attitudes in the modern, Western world. Jesus' simple homily delivered to a crowd of teenage students arguably changed the course of history.

He summed up the talk to this point with a remarkable challenge: "You therefore must be perfect, as your heavenly Father is perfect."[50] Clearly, this is not a law that can be kept. It's a goal, and a lofty one.

Jewish instruction recognized that some goals of the Law were beyond the ability of most people to achieve in a lifetime. Their attitude towards fulfilling such Law was, "You are not expected to complete the work, but neither are you free to refrain from it."[51] Jesus shared that attitude.

Jesus inculcated His students with the goal of representing God accurately. He later supplied the means by which they were able to achieve that goal, the Holy Spirit.[52] And His purpose for giving them that goal was that they would convey God's blessings to others.

---

[50] Matthew 5:48

[51] *Talmud*, Tractate *Avot* 2.16

[52] See Romans 8:4, Galatians 5:22-24

# Chapter 7: Who Is Your King?

| Outline of the Sermon on the Mount | |
| --- | --- |
| Subject: Life in the Kingdom of God | |
| | |
| I. God wants you to model His character... | Matthew 5 |
|   A. Ordinary believers are holy | (5:3-12) |
|   B. Your job is to demonstrate God's character | (5:13-16) |
|   C. The scriptures are your guide | (5:17-20) |
|   D. God's character is your standard | |
|     1. Hold relationships in highest esteem | (5:21-26) |
|     2. Keep your desires ordinate | (5:27-30) |
|     3. Speak truth at all times | (5:31-37) |
|     4. Do good to all, not evil | (5:38-48) |
| II. ...so give Him your whole-hearted devotion... | Matthew 6-7:2 |
|   A. Serve God, not reputation | (6:1-18) |
|   B. Serve God, not wealth | (6:19-24) |
|   C. Serve God, not self | (6:25-7:2) |
| III. ...and He will produce His character in you. | Matthew 7:3-27 |
|   A. Stay humble | (7:3-6) |
|   B. Pray for God's help | (7:7-12) |
|   C. Be diligent | (7:13-14) |
|   D. Stick to the Master's training | (7:15-23) |
|   E. He will make you unshakable | (7:24-27) |

Rabbi Jesus instructing His students to love their enemies was the first hinge point of the sermon. Jesus pivoted from explaining their goal—mimicking the character of God—to giving them the pattern by which they could reach it. As a starting point, they were to reach it through absolute, whole-hearted devotion to God. Trusting God was Plan A, and there was to be no Plan B.

There was nothing new about that. It's good, old-fashioned Jewish theology. I've heard plenty of Christians speaking of Jesus' answer regarding the greatest commandment of the Law[1] as though He were giving them something new, but in fact there were no Jews anywhere, then or now, who would not agree that the *Shema* was the greatest commandment:

> Hear, O Israel! YHWH is our God, YHWH alone! You shall love YHWH your God with all your heart and all your soul and all your might.[2]

The dispute in Judaism was over what was the second greatest commandment, which is why in every place in the gospels where Jesus was asked "What is the greatest commandment?" He answered with both the greatest and second greatest commandments. The point of that dispute was to understand which command took precedence when commands came into conflict.

For example, if your neighbor's ox fell into a pit, "love your neighbor as yourself"[3] meant that you had to help him get the animal out of the pit (not to mention that Exodus 23:4 and Deuteronomy 22:4 spelled that out). And of course, every Jew was to remember the Sabbath to keep it holy.[4]

But what if the animal fell into a pit on the Sabbath? In that case, good Jews were going to have to disobey one of those commands; either they would violate the Sabbath to help their neighbor rescue the animal, or they would stand at the edge of the pit weeping for their neighbor's misfortune at losing an animal but refuse to help because it was the Sabbath.[5] They wanted to

---

[1] Matthew 22:35-40, Mark 12:28-31, Luke 10:25-28

[2] Deuteronomy 6:4-5, *Tanakh: The Holy Scriptures*, Philadelphia, The Jewish Publication Society, 1985. I substituted "YHWH" for the conventional "LORD" indicating the use of the Name.

[3] Leviticus 19:18

[4] Exodus 20:8, Deuteronomy 5:12

know which disobedience God would forgive because they were obeying a higher law.

The House of Hillel, disciples of the great Rabbi Hillel, taught like Jesus that "love your neighbor as yourself" was the second greatest commandment. The House of Shammai taught that "remember the Sabbath" was the second greatest. This was one of more than three hundred conflicts between the houses of Hillel and Shammai in the *Talmud*.[6] In the New Testament, several of those conflicts show up, and Rabbi Jesus sided with the House of Hillel in all but one, which I mentioned in the section discussing divorce in the last chapter: Jesus rejected Hillel's interpretation of Deuteronomy 24:1.

## Hinting

The fact that the New Testament supplies only a fragment of the *Shema* in those passages illustrates something very important about how the Rabbis communicated with their disciples: they would provide only hints at the passages they were citing, but would seldom quote the entire passage.

The Jewish culture of the first century CE took for granted a level of knowledge of *Tanakh* that made it possible for Rabbis to convey entire passages by quoting just a tiny fragment of a reference. This is still common in Rabbinic teaching; they refer to a phrase, but intend the meaning conveyed by the entire passage. They expect their students to know by heart the rest of the passage that they're quoting.

---

[5] Jesus, Himself, used this dilemma in Luke 13:15 and Luke 14:5.

[6] http://www.jewishencyclopedia.com/articles/3190-bet-hillel-and-bet-shammai. Historically, the House of Shammai supported the violent rebellions against the Romans and was discredited when those failed, so modern *halakha* mostly supports the positions taken by the House of Hillel.

Jesus' sayings in the gospels are full of these sorts of references. For example, when Jesus quoted to the chief priests a sentence from Psalm 8, "Out of the mouth of infants and nursing babies you have prepared praise,"[7] He probably meant to say to them the very next phrase from the same Psalm, which reads "because of your foes, to still the enemy and the avenger." He wasn't just saying "Hey, it's ok for the children to praise in this manner," he was reminding the priests that by objecting to their praise they were siding with God's enemies. The priests, knowing *Tanakh* as well as Jesus, would have heard the rebuke loud and clear. The writer of Matthew's gospel also understood the rebuke, which is why he felt that the story was important enough to include but did not feel the need to explain it. Western readers, knowing very little of the Old Testament and not knowing the ways of the Rabbis, usually miss the point.

A more profound example shows up in John's gospel in the story of the woman caught in adultery, John 8:1-11.[8] John 7 reports an incident in which Rabbi Jesus had stood up at the annual Living Water festival, the last day of *Succoth*, and declared that the ceremony was pointing to Him.[9] The reaction of the crowd, reported in John 7, was all over the map, but apparently some Pharisees took it upon themselves to expose this boastful Rabbi Jesus as a fraud and make it clear that He was not, as He was claiming, the fountain of living waters.

They devised a trap for Rabbi Jesus: they would bring him an adulteress because the Law says that adulteresses should be stoned.[10] Only, Roman law did not permit the Jews to execute

---

[7] Matthew 21:16b, citing Psalm 8:2 from the Septuagint.

[8] Many modern scholars believe that John 7:53-8:11 was not part of the original gospel of John because those verses do not appear in the earliest manuscripts. I agreed with them until I saw the connection between that section and the Living Water ceremony. Now I suspect that the section was moved to its current location by somebody who had learned about the incident from an eyewitness and understood the connection.

[9] John 7:37-52.

prisoners without Roman oversight, so stoning an adulteress would have been called a riot and the leader of the riot—Jesus, in this case—would have been executed. If, on the other hand, the Rabbi refused to punish the adulteress they could accuse Him of destroying the Law of Moses and discredit Him.

So, they "caught" a woman in the act of adultery, at a moment's notice. That was a fraud in itself. They could not have done that if they hadn't known all along who among them was committing adultery with whom, and where and when they would meet. The affair was apparently common knowledge and they had done nothing about it.

Jesus, of course, understood this, and He also understood why they were doing it—they were scandalized by His calling Himself the source of living waters. So He gave them an incredibly pointed hint: he stooped down and started writing in the dirt.

There is only one place in *Tanakh* where that appears. It's in Jeremiah 17, just after the place where YHWH declares, "I, YHWH, search the heart and test the mind, to give every man according to his ways...."[11] A few verses later, in Jeremiah 17:13, it says

> ...those who turn away from You shall be written in the earth, for they have forsaken YHWH, the fountain of living waters.

The men watching Jesus performing this simple act, who knew the scriptures as well as He did, would have recognized the Rabbi identifying Himself again as the fountain of living waters, along with His accusation that by refusing His claim they were turning away from YHWH. Worse, they would have heard Him reminding them, from verse 10 in the same chapter, that YHWH

---

[10] It also says that adulterers should be stoned, Leviticus 20:10. I'm guessing that they wanted to simplify matters by bringing only the one person, but it's also possible that the adulterer was a friend of theirs.

[11] Jeremiah 17:10b

was watching their charade and judging their intent, which they knew to be corrupt. Jesus' next words, "Let him who is without sin among you be the first to throw a stone at her," they would have heard as a specific accusation: "Who's here that is not part of your plot?" None of them dared to throw a stone in the face of His correct accusation, so they left.

## The Devotion of Abram

Jesus dropped this same sort of hint into His discussion of loving enemies in a manner that modern interpreters miss entirely. It shows up most clearly in Luke's version of the lecture. Jesus had given them the implications of His instruction up front:

> But I say to you who hear, love your enemies, do good to those who hate you, bless those who curse you, pray for those who abuse you. To one who strikes you on the cheek, offer the other also, and from one who takes away your cloak do not withhold your tunic either. Give to everyone who begs from you, and from one who takes away your goods do not demand them back. And as you wish that others would do to you, do so to them.[12]

Then He posed a dilemma to them: if they only love their friends, they're doing no better than pagans do. And then He gave them the promise of reward:

> But love your enemies, and do good, and lend, expecting nothing in return, and your reward will be great, and you will be sons of the Most High, for he is kind to the ungrateful and the evil. Be merciful, even as your Father is merciful.[13]

Two phrases in his promise of reward point backwards to *Tanakh*. They occur side-by-side in the same sentence, and they both point to the same passage. Jesus' students would have

---

[12] Luke 6:27-31

[13] Luke 6:35-36

recognized both references and understood that what they were hearing was based on that story.

The first is the phrase, "your reward will be great." It recalls something that God, the Almighty, said to Abram in Genesis 15 after Abram tithed to Malchizedek in Genesis 14:

> After these things the word of the Lord came to Abram in a vision: "Fear not, Abram, I am your shield; your reward shall be very great."[14]

Hearing "your reward will be great," the disciples would have expected that what they were being told to do would earn for them the same reward that Abram had received because they were being told to do something similar to what he had done.

The second phrase that points us back to *Tanakh* is the title that Jesus used to describe God: "...you will be sons of the Most High." This is the only place in the gospels where Jesus used that title, "the Most High," for God. In Greek it's ὑψίστου, "hypsistou," but in Hebrew it would refer to "*El Elyon*," which translates in English to "the Most High God." And that, like the first phrase, recalls that same event in Genesis 14 and 15: Malchizedek was described as a priest of *El Elyon*, and Abram swore allegiance to *El Elyon*. Hearing that title would have confirmed to the disciples that they were hearing an exposition about Abram from Genesis 14 and 15.

As a young believer studying the Bible, it occurred to me to ask: where did Jesus get the things He taught? I had read through the Old Testament several times and had seen in it hardly any of the things that Jesus taught. I had the same questions about God's character revealed in the Old Testament that everybody else had. But Jesus, studying *Tanakh* among His Jewish brothers, developed all His wisdom and knowledge of God from life, study, and prayer. This implies that everything that Jesus taught

---

[14] Genesis 15:1

is available from *Tanakh* combined somehow with life experience, and that any of us, by prayer and study and with the help of the Holy Spirit, could learn what Jesus learned of God's character and intent by studying the same scriptures He studied.

The answer I hear most frequently when I bring this up is this: "He was God Incarnate. He knew everything."

That answer won't do at all. It is vitally important that we understand that Rabbi Jesus did everything He did during His ministry on earth using tools that are available to us as His disciples. To think otherwise is to place ourselves in an impossible dilemma: we are His *talmidim*, but we cannot possibly become just like Him because He used powers not available to us.[15] It's a convenient excuse for failure, of course, but the Apostles did not give us such comfort. Jesus was to have been the first of many like Him,[16] we are being transformed into His image,[17] and we're supposed to do the same works that He did.[18]

The hypostatic union[19] is a mystery, but however it worked, it did not give Jesus all the power of deity—omniscience, omnipotence, omnipresence—during His earthly ministry. Jesus clearly was not omnipresent; the gospel accounts are filled with markers pointing to His whereabouts.[20] Nor was He omnipotent; though He did remarkable works, He did them by power supplied to Him by the

---

[15] I discuss the goal of *talmidim* to become like their Rabbi in chapter nine.

[16] Romans 8:29

[17] II Corinthians 3:18

[18] John 14:12

[19] The hypostatic union is the doctrine that Jesus had two natures, one human and one divine. It was made a formal doctrine of the faith at the Council of Chalcedon in 451 CE. See https://www.theopedia.com/hypostatic-union.

[20] See, for instance, John 7:1. He was in Galilee; He was not in Judea. If He were omnipresent, He would have been present at all possible points in both Galilee and Judea, and everywhere else as well. Therefore, Jesus during His ministry could not have been omnipresent. The Father, however, is everywhere, and always has been.

Father through the Holy Spirit.[21] Nor, finally, was He omniscient; He obtained information the same way any of us might, and He lacked information about specific things.[22] He spent weeks on end praying for revelation and closeness with His Father,[23] and He prayed specifically before major changes in His ministry, suggesting that the actions He took after praying were His response to revelation or encouragement received during those times of prayer.[24]

So the question stands: where in *Tanakh* did Jesus learn about the character of the Father, and where can we do likewise?

Jesus just gave us two clues, both pointing to Genesis 14 and 15.

Genesis 14 tells a story about how some major kings from the areas that we now call Iran and Iraq took tribute from all over the Fertile Crescent. The story points to a cluster of five small cities located near the Dead Sea that were among those paying tribute to the Iranian kings.

---

[21] See, for instance, John 5:19: "…the Son can do nothing of his own accord, but only what he sees the Father doing." Or consider Mark 3:23-30, where Jesus calls it "blasphemy against the Holy Spirit" to attribute Jesus' own healings to a demonic source, implying that He did His healings by the Holy Spirit.

[22] See, for example, Matthew 24:36: "But concerning that day and hour no one knows, not even the angels of heaven, nor the Son, but the Father only."

[23] See Matthew 4:1-11 and Luke 4:1-13, for a clear example. All that the text reveals about why He fasted forty days was "to be tempted by the devil," but that was just the writer's description of the event, not Jesus' motive for fasting. Since Jesus went to fast and pray after hearing a voice from heaven announcing "You are My Beloved Son" (Mark 1:11) , and since the tempter taunted Him twice with "If you are the son of God, you should do X," we can infer that Jesus was praying regarding a question something like this: "Ok, I'm the Son of God. What does a Son of God do?" He had received a job title, and was asking for the job description.

[24] Examples include Matthew 4:1-11 before the beginning of His Galilean ministry, Luke 6:1 before selecting His Apostles, Luke 9:28-36 before setting His face to go to Jerusalem to be crucified, and of course the prayer in Gethsemane, Matthew 26:36-46, before His arrest.

Abram lived near those five, small cities, in the hills west of the Dead Sea among the Amorites, near what later became Hebron. His nephew Lot had parted with him because their herds of animals had become too large to graze in the same place. Lot had settled in one of those cities, Sodom.

The kings of those five cities decided one year to stop paying tribute. Maybe they thought that their combined tribute would have been worth less than the cost and trouble of trying to enforce it from as far away as Iran. Whatever their reasons were, the king of *Elam* (northern Iran) did not agree. The next year he came to punish the rebellious kings with his allies from *Shinar* (Babylon), *Ellasar* (on the east bank of the Euphrates River south and east of Babylon), and *Goyim* (the word simply means "nations" in Hebrew, and nobody is sure to which ancient city this refers.) They followed a path that took them south along the east bank of the Jordan River, stopping to gather plunder from cities along the way, until they reached the northern end of the Arabian Desert. Then they turned around and came back to deal with Sodom, Gomorrah, and their allies.

The four kings from the east won their battle against the five kings from the Dead Sea area and took the people of the five cities captive. They also took plunder from those cities, and verse 11 of Genesis 14 adds that they took Sodom's food supply (this becomes relevant later.) They also took Lot and his family, and headed north, probably along the path on which they came, east of the Jordan.

Abram was a fairly powerful king in his own right. He already had trained an army from the men of his own household and he was aided by his Amorite neighbors, Mamre, Eshcol, and Aner. When Abram learned that Lot had been taken, he mobilized his small army and traveled north, probably along the west bank of the Jordan, until he intercepted the conquerors somewhere near the modern, southern border of Lebanon and chased them to near

Damascus, in Syria. In all he traveled about 200 miles north to rescue Lot.

Abram defeated the king of Elam and his allies. When he returned from rescuing Lot, Abram had in his possession all the goods from all the towns that the Iranian kings had captured— and they had plundered pretty much the entire east side of the Jordan valley. By Bronze Age rules, he was entitled to keep all those goods, and also to keep all the captured people as his slaves or vassals. And in a very real sense, since those foreign kings that he'd beaten were the ruling powers in the Ancient Near East at the time, Abram had every right to call himself the king of the known world. He might even have chosen to visit Elam himself and sack it if he dared to try.

But that's not what he did.

Genesis 14 and 15 record three conversations that took place when Abram returned from rescuing his nephew, Lot:

1) Malchizedek, priest of *El Elyon*, blessed Abram, and Abram tithed to Malchizedek in reply (Gen 14:18-20, 22-23).

2) The king of Sodom bargained with Abram to get his people back, but Abram unexpectedly returned all of Sodom's goods to the king of Sodom (Gen 14:17, 21-24).

3) God declared that He would be Abram's provider, and that all the nations would be blessed in him (Gen 15:1-6).

The third conversation actually continues to the end of chapter 15. In this continuation, God made a solemn covenant with Abram which committed Him to do remarkable things for Abram's descendants. However, the continuation is not strictly relevant to our subject here, so I'll tell that story another day.

The first and third conversations are two sides of a suzerainty pact between Abram and YHWH. "Suzerainty" refers to a pact made between a greater king and a lesser one. The lesser king pays homage and protection money to the greater king, and in return the greater king agrees to protect the lesser king.

The first conversation gets reported to us like this:

> And Melchizedek king of Salem brought out bread and wine. (He was priest of God Most High.) And he blessed him and said,
>
>> "Blessed be Abram by God Most High,
>> Possessor of heaven and earth;
>> and blessed be God Most High,
>> who has delivered your enemies into your hand!"
>
> And Abram gave him a tenth of everything.[25]

Melchizedek, as priest, claimed to be representing *El Elyon*, which gets translated here as "God Most High." Most gods in the Bronze Age were local and tribal; they ruled within limited areas. Melchizedek made a point of saying that this *El Elyon* owned everything, not just on earth but also in heaven. Melchizedek's God was the God above all other gods, the Most High God. Those blessed by his God would be blessed above all other earthly kings, who served lesser gods. Melchizedek let Abram know that he'd succeeded in beating those great kings from the east only because *El Elyon* had blessed him.

Abram had come to that part of the world on the command of a god he knew as YHWH. YHWH had told Abram in Haran (southern Turkey) to travel to Canaan, where YHWH said that He would give Abram land. So it was reasonable for Abram to think that YHWH held influence in both those places, and probably also in Ur, where YHWH had called Abram's father,

---

[25] Genesis 14:18-20

Terah.[26] In other words, YHWH was not just local, He was universal.

On reasoning something like this, Abram recognized Melchizedek's *El Elyon* as the same God who had been leading him. We know this because when he spoke to the King of Sodom in verse 22, he called God "YHWH *El Elyon* (YHWH the Most High God), possessor of heaven and earth," combining the names that both he and Melchizedek were using for God, and adding Melchizedek's description that declared how this God ruled everything.

Melchizedek had brought bread and wine in order to make a pact; they make treaties by eating together in that part of the world. So Abram embraced Melchizedek's offer and ate with him, and then declared himself the vassal of *El Elyon* by paying to *El Elyon's* priest a tenth of everything he had just captured. The tithe was the king's portion in the ancient world; when a king returned from conquest with plunder, he took ten percent and would divide the other ninety percent among his followers. You can see echoes of this in Samuel's description of what a king would demand of the Israelites in I Samuel 8:15 and 17. By tithing, Abram was saying to Melchizedek's God, "You are my king, and I am Your vassal. I trust You to protect me and provide for me."

In the third of the three conversations (I'll deal with the second conversation below), God responded to Abram, "I will be your shield,"[27] which is what the greater king said to the vassal king in a suzerainty agreement. He went further to assure Abram that he would not be sorry to have accepted His protection: "Your

---

[26] Genesis 11:31. It does not say specifically that YHWH called Terah. However, Terah set out for Canaan just like Abram did, and combining verse 28 with verse 31b, it looks as though Terah allowed himself to be diverted by his brokenness over the loss of his son Haran. Thus Terah may have been called by YHWH, and may have had the opportunity to become what Abraham became: the source of the blessing for all nations.

[27] Genesis 15:1b

reward will be very great." Abram's reward turned out to be the answer to the deepest cry of his heart, his desire for sons—a cry that no other sovereign would have been able to fulfill. God promised Abram more sons than he could count. All modern Jews represent the fulfillment of that reward, and in a sense all modern Christians do, too.[28]

In the second of the three conversations, the king of Sodom came to Abram to bargain for his life. He didn't know what Abram was going to do with him or his people—make them slaves to cut wood and carry water, sacrifice them to his gods, or whatever, but he clearly feared for his life and the lives of his people. So he pleaded with Abram, "Just let us go. You can keep all our stuff."

Abram faced a clear and solemn choice. He could have kept all the goods he had won by conquest. He could have kept the people, too, as his slaves. He could have been the King of the World. Or, he could honor his suzerainty pact with *El Elyon* and forego all that. By trusting God completely and giving Him his full devotion, Abram was able to treat enormous riches and power as secondary. His level of trust in YHWH gave him liberty to be generous with the king of Sodom.

So Abram did something unexpected; he gave up most of the wealth he could have kept. He'd sworn to make YHWH his source, so he told the king of Sodom, "Here, take your stuff." Abram said that he was trusting YHWH *El Elyon* to provide for his needs, so he did not want to take even a thread from the King of Sodom. "Lest you should say, 'I have made Abram rich'" was Abram's way of saying "*El Elyon* is my provider, and you are not."

Most likely Abram also returned the goods of the other cities that had been sacked, and set those kings and people free as well. The passage does not say so, but that would be consistent with the theme of the story.

---

[28] This is the lesson in Galatians 3:6-29.

Just letting them go with their things was gracious enough, but it turns out that by doing so Abram saved a lot of lives. The "stuff" included Sodom's food supply, as was noted in Genesis 14:11. If Abram had kept all the stuff, the Sodomites would have had to raid surrounding towns to steal food for the entire next year, or they would have starved to death. So Abram actually prevented a year's worth of murderous raiding by being generous.

## Jesus' Lesson from Abram

Out of this act of generosity arising from Abram's commitment to YHWH *El Elyon*, Jesus first pulled the following list of behaviors:

- Love your enemies.

- Do good to those who hate you.

- Bless those who curse you.

- Pray for those who abuse you.

- Give to those who beg, and expect nothing in return.

- Don't resist evil people; don't hit back, don't counter-sue.

- Be righteous like God, who makes the sun shine on the righteous and the wicked alike.

The passage in Genesis does not bring up the wickedness of the King of Sodom, nor does it make him out to be Abram's enemy. But just turning forward a few pages in Genesis takes us to where Jesus might have found that: the Sodomites were so wicked that God sent fire from heaven to destroy their city. And it was to these remarkably wicked people that Abram returned their goods with his blessing and allowed them to go back to their lives as before.

This clearly made a strong impression on Rabbi Jesus, who used it as a broad model of conduct. Abram did not actually do all those things for the King of Sodom, but Jesus took the hint and taught how his students might behave if they had the same attitude. Jesus taught, "If your devotion to YHWH is complete like Abram's was, you should be able to do all these things for the less holy people around you. Your conduct toward them should arise out of your confidence that your own needs will be met by your Sovereign God."

But Jesus drew more than those things from Abram's story. The entire sixth chapter of Matthew's gospel was Jesus' exposition on Abram's devotion. His disciples were to be devoted to YHWH in the same way that Abram was devoted to YHWH, trusting Him to meet all their needs in response to their trust just as He had met Abram's needs—needs for recognition, provision, and security.

It was no accident that Jesus chose Abram to illustrate the devotion He wanted to teach his students. God's purpose for Israel began with Abram, and we've seen in Matthew 5:13-16 how Jesus recognized that that purpose had been derailed. If Jesus was planting a Church that would successfully complete Israel's mission to redeem the nations, it had to begin by going back to Abram and reasserting what had been intended from the beginning. If Jesus was going to teach His disciples to fulfill God's call to bless all the nations, He had to show them what it was that God loved so much about Abram in the first place.

Genesis 15 is where the writer says of Abram that he "believed YHWH, and He credited it to him as righteousness."[29] Later on, Paul, the Apostle, would use that declaration to describe what God wanted of those who embraced the Messiah.[30] Believers in the Messiah were to imitate the faithfulness and complete devotion that Abram had shown there in Genesis 14. Jesus was making the same point: imitating Abram's complete trust in God was to be the basis for all Christian godliness. This devotion,

---

[29] Genesis 15:6

[30] See Romans 4, particularly verse 3. See also Galatians 3 and 4, particularly 3:6.

echoed in the *Shema* as "love YHWH with all your heart, soul, and strength," is the very core of what God expects from His people, both then and now.

It is vitally important that we notice, not just the devotion that Abram gave YHWH, but the provision that YHWH gave him in reply. Jesus spent very little time in the Sermon on the Mount explaining God's role in producing righteousness in His disciples, but that role was present and very clear to them. The rest of the sermon spelled out things that the disciples needed to do in order to become adequate representatives of YHWH's holiness, but underlying every word of it was the presence of YHWH, Himself, infusing their every choice and act with His grace and power, enabling them to do what Israel had not been able to do 'til then.

That's why Jesus repeated seven times in the early verses of Matthew 6 the fact that they would obtain a reward from YHWH by their devotion. It is also why Jesus gave instructions regarding prayer in this context. The source of their devotion, and the source of the righteousness that would result from their devotion, and even the reward for their devotion, was YHWH, Himself.

Jesus' seven-fold mention of the reward for doing good deeds in secret might have been viewed as being just a little bit vulgar by the Rabbis of His day. In *Pirkei Avot* ("the Wisdom of the Fathers," another name for tractate *Avot* in the *Talmud*), a Jewish sage from almost 200 years before Jesus was quoted as saying,

> Do not be as servants who are serving the master in order to receive a reward, rather be as servants who are serving the master not in order to receive a reward; and may the fear of Heaven be upon you.[31]

Other Rabbis in the *Talmud* did recognize that some conduct merited rewards or punishments from God, so we know that such

---

[31] *Talmud*, Tractate *Avot* 1.3

thoughts were not forbidden, but they probably regarded doing things specifically for the purpose of earning a reward to be less than perfect.

In this context, Jesus did not seem to care. His lesson pointed to the outcome of Abram's devotion, which was God meeting his heart's greatest need and using Abram to fulfill His plan to redeem the nations. The message Jesus was conveying to His students appears to have been, "Do what Abram did, and you will get what Abram got. Mimic Abram's devotion and you can fulfill Abram's destiny."

## Enemies of Devotion

The specific point that Jesus made in Matthew 5:43 through the end of Matthew 6 was about who was to be king. Were His *talmidim* going to serve *El Elyon*, the Owner of Heaven and Earth, and trust His provision? Or were they going to count on the King of Sodom to make them rich?

Jesus listed three things in their culture to which people commonly gave their devotion, things that would distract His students from receiving the reward God wanted to give them. "Serve God, not reputation. Serve God, not wealth. Serve God, not self."

Serve God, serve God, serve God. Seek first the kingdom of God. You can only have one Master. Serve Him. The message was pretty clear.

The first enemy was reputation:

> Beware of practicing your righteousness before other people in order to be seen by them, for then you will have no reward from your Father who is in heaven.[32]

---

[32] Matthew 6:1

He repeated this basic lesson three times concerning three different religious acts: giving to the needy (Matthew 6:2-4), praying (Matthew 6:5-7), and fasting (Matthew 6:16-18). Jesus pointed out a major thing that tempts those who perform religious obligations: they do them "to be seen by [other people]."

Without thinking carefully we might get confused by the fact that God selected His people, the Jews, to be an example of holiness to be seen by other nations, and that Jesus was planting a kingdom that employed the same strategy. How is that not "performing righteousness before others in order to be seen by them?" The answer is that the first is God's purpose, and the second is ours. God's reason for blessing a people may be for the other nations to see and learn, but that does not mean that each individual ought to do what he does for the purpose of building up his own reputation before his friends and neighbors.

Jesus gave instructions about prayer here that I will discuss in the next chapter. For the moment, notice only that His concern in Matthew 6:7-8 was different from his concern in Matthew 6:1-6 and 6:16-17; it was not about praying to be seen by other people, but about praying without understanding the character of God. Where some religious Jews were apparently guilty of showing off, Gentiles were simply ignorant about how to approach God because they did not know Him.

Regarding doing "righteousness," Jesus said the same things three times. The triple repetition would have been taken as strong emphasis. He said this:

- If you perform for the crowd, only the crowd will reward you. "Truly I say to you, they have received their reward." Their reward was attention—and nothing else.

- If you perform for God, God will reward you.

It's the same choice Abram faced: will you receive your reward from YHWH, or from the King of Sodom? Jesus drew on the clear advantage of having a patron Who could do what no other sovereign could do, as Abram discovered.

The next enemy of devotion that Jesus mentioned was money, and His lesson was the same: "You can serve God, or you can serve money, but you can't serve both. Which will it be?" *El Elyon*, or the King of Sodom?

By now we should be comfortable with Jesus' habit of exaggerating for effect, so nobody should mistake "do not lay up for yourselves treasures on earth" (Matthew 6:19) as a command not to have savings accounts. The Rabbi's concern was clearly about what we value most. Jesus did a fair amount of teaching about money,[33] suggesting that it was a useful servant. Here He stated the other side of the coin: though money makes a useful servant, it makes a poor master.

"The eye is the lamp of the body" (6:22) is an expression that mystifies some modern readers, but it's actually straightforward. Light meant knowledge, and darkness meant ignorance or confusion. Jesus was directing His students to value YHWH. If their desire was consistently toward the Father, He would grant them understanding. If their desire wandered onto temporal things, they would live without understanding and die without reward. "If the light that is in you is darkness, how great is the darkness" (6:23) declares the horrible condition in which some people find themselves, where the things they value most have no real value at all, and they live entirely worthless lives because of their devotion to those things. The Apostle Paul taught the same lesson in Romans 8:5-8, Romans 12:2, Galatians 5:16-24, and Colossians 3:1-2, as the war between flesh and Spirit. "It is the

---

[33] One estimate I read suggested that one out of ten verses in the gospels discuss money. I don't know whether that's accurate or not, but there are certainly plenty of verses that illustrate Jesus' familiarity with the topic. My favorites include Luke 16:9-13, which appears to be additional explanation for Jesus' notions about serving Mammon, and Luke 14:28-30.

Spirit who gives life; the flesh is no help at all," taught Rabbi Jesus.[34]

Jesus then addressed anxiety, which arises from self-centeredness. His message was that YHWH is trustworthy and understands our needs, so we need not worry about money if we trust Him. "Seek the kingdom of God and His righteousness first, and all the things you need will be added to you".[35]

The Psalms support His confidence in God's commitment to meeting the needs of all His creatures:

> The eyes of all look to you,
> and you give them their food in due season.
> You open your hand;
> you satisfy the desire of every living thing.
> The LORD is righteous in all his ways
> and kind in all his works.
> The LORD is near to all who call on him,
> to all who call on him in truth.
> He fulfills the desire of those who fear him;
> he also hears their cry and saves them.[36]

However, we should not ignore the fact that instead of quoting the Psalms, Jesus offered examples from nature—the birds of the air and the flowers of the field. We already know that Jesus believed and endorsed the scriptures, but He had no objection at all to teaching about God's character from the world that He created. You and I, as his disciples, should feel free to do the same; both nature and scripture were composed by the same Author.

Notice, also, that the Gentiles got a second mention here. As when He was talking about public praying, Jesus did not chide

---

[34] John 6:63a

[35] Matthew 6:33, my paraphrase.

[36] Psalm 145:15-19

Gentiles for low character but simply pointed out that they behaved as though they did not know God's ways. He expected His students to know better. "The Gentiles seek after these things, and your heavenly Father knows that you need them all."[37] Because Jesus did not expect Gentiles to know God's character, He sometime expressed surprise when He met Gentiles who did, in fact, understand His ways.[38]

## Don't Judge

Most readers accept the chapter boundary and consider Jesus' next instruction, "Judge not, that you be not judged," to be a new topic.[39] They lump that together with "Why do you see the speck that is in your brother's eye, but do not notice the log that is in your own eye?" But when we look at Luke's gospel, we find that those are separate comments from separate topics. Luke's version groups "Don't judge" with giving generously, which one might naturally associate with Jesus' warning against serving money:

> Judge not, and you will not be judged; condemn not, and you will not be condemned; forgive, and you will be forgiven; give, and it will be given to you. Good measure, pressed down, shaken together, running over, will be put into your lap. For with the measure you use it will be measured back to you."[40]

The connection between judging and giving is that they are opposites. You cannot be generous in the manner that Abram was generous toward those that you judge and condemn. If Abram had judged the King of Sodom he might not have returned his goods to him, thinking that he did not deserve them back. Jesus

---

[37] Matthew 6:32

[38] See, for example, Matthew 8:5-13, Matthew 15:21-28, Luke 17:18

[39] Matthew 7:1

[40] Luke 6:37-38

taught His students to be generous in forgiveness and gracious acts as well as in money and goods.

The connection between judging and the question, "Who is your king?" is obvious: it's the king's prerogative to judge His servants. If you're not the king, you don't get to judge the king's servants. That's why Jesus raised "Don't judge" in this context, an exposition regarding who was to be king.

A lot of us need to hear this. A great deal of Church teaching about Matthew 7:1-2 focuses on reasons not to obey Jesus. This happens because non-believers love to quote Matthew 7:1 to stop Christians from calling things "sin" that they want to do without remorse (mostly illicit sex). In reaction, Christian teachers rush to defend their habit of naming sins—and end up justifying judging their fellow-Christians because they're not careful. One popular teacher loves to say, "Jesus was not saying not to judge, He was teaching us how to judge." He then resorts to John 7:24, "Do not judge by appearances, but judge with right judgment," which is not a command to believers at all, but gets ripped entirely out of context and used to soften the clear instruction in Matthew 7:1.

This deflecting of "Don't judge" is a bit confused. I agree that non-believers are usually misusing Jesus' words when they quote that passage, but that is no reason to ignore Him. He had a point, and it was not "Judge your brothers righteously."

There are three, different words translated "judge" in the New Testament, and Jesus forbade us to do only one of them. Jesus said "Don't κρίνω ('krino,' to pass judgment on the words or deeds of others)." This is the sort of authoritative declaration that God will do to all humans on the Last Day. In most places in the New Testament we are advised that *krino* is God's job and that the wise course is to leave that job in His hands, particularly when it's our fellow-Christians we are tempted to judge.[41] The ruling principle in these cases is always the same: He's God, and

---

[41] See, for example, I Corinthians 4:5, Romans 14:10-13, James 4:10-11.

we're not. Those other Christians don't serve us, they serve Him. He gets to judge them. We don't.

We are, on the other hand, instructed to discern good from evil—for ourselves and our local church-mates. When speaking of such matters, Paul, the Apostle, used the words διακρίνω ("*diakrino*," to make a distinction or decide a dispute) or ἀνακρίνω ("*anakrino*," to evaluate in a forensic or official fashion). For instance, Paul said that when sharing the Lord's Supper we are supposed to *diakrino* the Body rightly, and then we will not receive *krino* from God.[42] He also chided the Corinthian believers, "Can it be that there is no one among you wise enough to *diakrino* between the brothers...?"[43] And he told them, "The spiritual person *anakrinos* all things, but is himself to be *anakrinoed* by no one."[44]

There are also times when *diakrino* is a bad idea; see James 1:6, Mark 11:23, and Romans 14:23, where *diakrino* gets translated "doubt."

All the places where we are instructed not to *krino* address how we treat one another in the fellowship of the Church, the kingdom of God. Simply put, we are to make moral assessments so that we know how to conduct ourselves, but we are not to pronounce judgment on other believers. Judging the believers is not our job, because other believers are not our property. We all belong to God, and He will judge us all. There is no need to ignore this clear prohibition while explaining to non-believers, when it becomes necessary, that sin is sin.

"Don't judge" was the second hinge point in the sermon. The last major segment of the Sermon on the Mount speaks of students committing to learn from their teachers. Judging other students is

---

[42] I Corinthians 11:29,31

[43] I Corinthians 6:5b

[44] I Corinthians 2:15. Please pardon my using English suffixes on Greek verbs.

one of the pitfalls that students experience, as we'll see in chapter nine.

Luke's version correctly places Jesus' jest about "the log in your own eye" into this discussion of teachers and students. This is the next major point in the outline of Jesus' sermon. There's a process of learning that students need to face if they are to mirror God's character properly. That's the rest of Matthew 7, but before we go there we need to talk about prayer.

# Chapter 8: Confident Prayer

## Outline of the Sermon on the Mount
### Subject: Life in the Kingdom of God

| | |
|---|---|
| I. God wants you to model His character... | Matthew 5 |
|     A. Ordinary believers are holy | (5:3-12) |
|     B. Your job is to demonstrate God's character | (5:13-16) |
|     C. The scriptures are your guide | (5:17-20) |
|     D. God's character is your standard | |
|         1. Hold relationships in highest esteem | (5:21-26) |
|         2. Keep your desires ordinate | (5:27-30) |
|         3. Speak truth at all times | (5:31-37) |
|         4. Do good to all, not evil | (5:38-48) |
| | |
| II. ...so give Him your whole-hearted devotion... | Matthew 6-7:2 |
|     A. Serve God, not reputation | (6:1-18) |
|     B. Serve God, not wealth | (6:19-24) |
|     C. Serve God, not self | (6:25-7:2) |
| | |
| III. ...and He will produce His character in you. | Matthew 7:3-27 |
|     A. Stay humble | (7:3-6) |
|     **B. Pray for God's help** | **(7:7-12)** |
|     C. Be diligent | (7:13-14) |
|     D. Stick to the Master's training | (7:15-23) |
|     E. He will make you unshakable | (7:24-27) |

The last leg of the Sermon on the Mount, most of Matthew chapter 7, is about students and teachers. Rabbi Jesus, having set His students to the task of representing God accurately, and having explained how they could only do that if they were whole-heartedly devoted to God, proceeded to discuss the process of becoming the good examples that they were called to be. He focused on humility.

But underlying this process, Jesus understood that ultimately it was the power of God, the Father, which would produce His character in His students. Recognizing that, Jesus taught prayer in the middle of His warning against approval-seeking, in the form of the Lord's Prayer.[1] He taught it again in the middle of His explanation about how to be the right kind of student, in Matthew 7. The subject of the prayers was different in these two passages, but Jesus was teaching the same principle in both. His purpose in bringing it up was to direct His students to place their confidence, neither in their ability as students, nor in His ability as teacher, but in God the Father, whose work the instruction really was. And His specific point was that when they asked God for what they needed, they should expect Him to answer "Yes."

## Jewish Prayers

Jewish prayer was usually more cautious than that. Regular prayer was an important part of their relationship with God the Almighty, but most of them would have considered it presumptuous to expect God to give them what they asked every time.

Jewish prayer in the first century contained both pre-written prayers and off-the-cuff requests. On the liturgical side, the Men of the Great Assembly had written eighteen prayers for daily recitation that the Jews called *shemonei esrai* ("eighteen blessings").[2] These were to be recited three times a day, morning, afternoon, and evening. (Several other prayers have been added to the daily liturgy since then, including one thanking God that they're not heretics like the Christians. I don't recommend that one.) Modern Jews call this set of prayers the *Amidah*; *Amidah*

---

[1] Matthew 6:9-14

[2] "A hundred and twenty elders, that is, the Men of the Great Assembly... established the eighteen blessings of the *Amida* in their fixed order, which also shows that the order of these blessings may not be changed." *Talmud*, Tractate *Megillah* 17b.

simply means "standing," and that name was used because in modern Judaism the prayers are supposed to be offered while standing in the synagogue facing the ark containing the Torah, which is open so that the people can see the scrolls.

The eighteen begin with praising God for revealing Himself to the patriarchs (Abraham, Isaac, and Jacob), for being good to all including the weak, the sick, the fallen, and the poor, for His holiness, and for granting wisdom. They proceed to ask Him to return His people to His service, to forgive their sins, both intended and accidental, to redeem and restore Israel, and to heal and save them. Then they ask for a year of abundant produce. They ask that God restore the judges of Israel, gather the exiles, restore the House of David (which amounts to calling for the Messiah), restore the temple and return to Zion. They call for God's blessing on the righteous, the pious, the elders, the teachers, and all Israel. They pray (in circular fashion) that their prayers be heard, and then they thank God for being their God and call for peace on Israel.

Jews regarded these prayers as vitally important. The *Mishna* contains a discussion over whether persons praying the daily prayers should allow themselves to be interrupted even if it's the King greeting them (one ignored oriental kings only at great risk) or a snake wrapping itself around their leg.[3] The sages recognized the possible dangers, but employing the same sort of hyperbole we've seen Jesus using so often, they made the point that interrupting the prayers was even more dangerous in its own way.

In the context discussing these prayers, one story in the *Mishna* tells how an exceptionally pious Rabbi, Hanina ben Dosa, put his foot on a snake's lair (apparently while praying) and when the snake bit him it died. He brought the snake to the *beth hamidrash* and told his students, "See, my sons, it is not the snake that kills, it is sin that kills!"[4]

---

[3] *Talmud*, Tractate *Berakhot* 32b-33a.

[4] *Talmud*, Tractate *Berakhot* 33a.

Setting the eighteen prayers of *shemonai esrai* next to the Lord's
Prayer from Matthew 6, we find a few differences arising from
Jesus' special calling, but nothing different from the Jewish
pattern. The standard Jewish set was longer, of course, but if we
take Jesus' prayer as a list of subject headings rather than a
prayer to be recited word for word, they're similar. Jesus' version
called for establishing the kingdom of God in place of calling for
the national restoration of Israel, reflecting the world-changing
importance of the arrival of the kingdom. He called for daily
bread rather than an abundant annual harvest, suggesting that
Jesus expected God to meet needs at a more immediate level. His
prayer for forgiveness included a reminder that they needed to
forgive others as well. And, He added a tag on the end calling his
students to ask that they be delivered from the evil one. But
despite those differences, Jews familiar with the *Amidah* find
nothing remarkable about the form of the Lord's Prayer. Matthew
6:9-13 is very much like standard, Jewish daily prayer.

In addition to the liturgy, Jewish scripture provides us with
examples of Jewish prayers made in the moment. We find Moses
falling on his face before God throughout the Torah, often
pleading for the Israelites when they sinned or complained. We
find Elijah and Elisha calling on God directly when they needed
Him to intervene. We find Daniel praying for the nation in Daniel
chapter 9. We see Jesus praying throughout the night on several
occasions, and His prayers in Gethsemane are recorded for us.
Impromptu prayers were normal and expected, and there were
few rules about them; one simply spoke from the heart in the
moment. Such prayers were considered an expression of the sort
of love for God that He commanded.[5]

---

[5] There's a brief, clear discussion of impromptu prayer as a *mitzvah* (a good
deed done as a religious duty) at
http://www.askmoses.com/en/article/577,2080045/Is-it-a-Mitzvah-
commandment-to-pray.html. It's modern, but I think it reflects a long-standing
attitude.

## God as Father and the *Khasidim*

The place where Jesus' instruction about prayer deviated from ordinary Jewish practice was His confidence that God would answer "yes." The first place in the Sermon on the Mount that this appears is the opening phrase of the Lord's Prayer, "Our Father."

Judaism did recognize and speak of God as Father, but usually He was father to the nation, Israel, not to individual Jews. This echoed God's directive to Pharaoh, "Israel is my firstborn son, and I say to you, 'Let my son go that he may serve me.'"[6] There are a couple of places in Deuteronomy where the Israelites are called God's children in a plural sense, but on the whole individuals calling God "father" are rare in the writings of the sages.[7]

That Jesus repeated the father-son relationship to His students so often reflects His goal of reconciling Man to God. Jesus had such a relationship Himself, and He was trying to impress into His students their stature in the eyes of God as His beloved children.

There are prayers from a handful of unusual Rabbis in the *Mishna* that show a relationship between men and God that was similar to what Jesus called for. The Jews called these Rabbis *Khasidim*, which translates to "pious ones," and they regarded them as special.[8] The *Khasidim* were miracle-workers something like Jesus, and they seemed to relate to God in a manner that fit

---

[6] Exodus 4:22

[7] Safrai, Shmuel, "Jesus and the Hasidim," *Jerusalem Perspective*, January/June 1994, No. 42, p. 6. The article may be downloaded from https://www.jerusalemperspective.com/2685/, but is behind a pay wall.

[8] The *Khasidim* in the *Mishna* are not to be confused with the modern movement that is called "Hasidic Judaism." The modern Hasidic movement was started by an eighteenth century Polish Rabbi named Israel Eliezer, called the Ba'al Shem-Tov. See http://www.jewishencyclopedia.com/articles/2252-ba-al-shem-tob-israel-b-eliezer. The modern group called *Chabad* descends from this movement.

Jesus' instruction. People used to seek out the *Khasidim* to ask for special needs like healing, deliverance from demons, rain during droughts, and so on.

A story in the *Mishna* about a Rabbi called Honi the Circle-Maker[9] shows how close they were to God. In this story, the people of Jerusalem came to Honi during a drought and asked him to pray for rain. Honi was so confident that his prayer would be answered that he warned them to bring their clay matzos-ovens indoors so they did not get ruined by the rainfall (it was the Passover season, during which little rainfall is expected). Then he stood outside the city, drew a circle around himself in the dirt, and prayed to God,

> "O Lord of the world, your children have turned their faces to me, for I am like a son of the house before you. I swear by your great name that I will not stir from here until you have pity on your children."

A drizzle began, and Honi prayed "Not for such rain have I prayed, but for rain that will fill the cisterns, pits, and caverns." Then a violent downpour began, and Honi prayed "Not for such rain have I prayed, but for rain of goodwill, blessing, and graciousness." Then it rained steadily for days, until the people came to Honi again and asked that he pray for it to stop raining.

The writers of the *Mishna* did not go out of their way to report miracles. The only reason this story was included was to illustrate a judge's choice not to execute the law against Honi.[10] He could have punished Honi because holding himself hostage to manipulate the Almighty was improper.

> Simeon ben Shetah sent to him, saying, "Had you not been Honi I would have pronounced a ban against you! But what shall I do to you? You importune God and he performs your will, like a son that importunes his father he performs his

---

[9] *Talmud*, Tractate *Taanit* 3.8.

[10] Safrai, op. cit., p. 10.

will. Of you the Scripture says, 'Let your father and your mother be glad, and let her that bore you rejoice.'"

In this story it appears that it was unusual for a relationship between a man and the Almighty to be like that of a child with his Father. Yet, the leaders responsible for enforcing the Law recognized the special status of a man whose conduct showed that he had such a relationship with God. Meanwhile, Honi seems to have known that it was not just he who had this relationship, because he called all the Israelites God's children.

In another story Rabbi Hanina ben Dosa, he of the dead snake, was studying Torah with another great Rabbi, Yohanan ben Zakkai.[11] The son of Yohanan fell ill, so he asked Hanina, "Pray for him so that he may live." Hanina put his head between his knees and prayed for him, and he lived. Rabbi Yohanan ben Zakkai remarked about himself that if he had put his head between his knees for an entire day God would not have taken notice. His wife asked him, "Is Hanina greater than Yohanan ben Zakkai?" Yohanan explained to her, "No, but he is like a trusted slave who can come to his master at any time, where I am like a high official in his court who can only come at appointed times."

I have heard Jews say similar things about the prophets. They recognize that prophets hold special status with God and understand that sometimes the Law gets suspended for those who live in this status.

This sort of special status plays a role in a story about a Rabbi named Yehoshua ben Levi.[12] A man named Ulla had fled to the town of Lod and the Romans were threatening to kill everybody in the town unless they handed him over. Yehoshua ben Levi, who used to get regular visits from the prophet Elijah (mystical visits; the prophet was long dead at this time), convinced Ulla to

---

[11] *Talmud*, Tractate *Berakhot* 5.5.

[12] Jerusalem *Talmud*, Tractate *Terumot* 8, Genesis *Rabbah* 94 (ed. Theodor-Albeck, p. 1184-1185), as cited in Safrai, op. cit., note 61, p. 20.

turn himself over to the Romans in order to spare the town, which was consistent with *halakha*. But Elijah stopped appearing to Yehoshua, so he spent many days fasting and seeking to understand why. Eventually Elijah reappeared to him and chided him, "Do you think I appear to informers?" Rabbi Yehoshua replied that he had simply been obeying *halakha*, but Elijah would have none of it: "Is that the *Mishna* of the *Khasidim*?" he asked, and explained that as one who walks closely with God, he should have ignored *halakha* and trusted that the Almighty would have intervened to save the town.

I supplied these stories because they illustrate what the Jews of Jesus' day considered special relationships between holy men and God (and also because they're entertaining). Jesus, though He was probably not a *Khasid* (the Hebrew singular of *Khasidim*) in any formal sense, was like them in His friendship with and close reliance on God.

## Expecting "Yes"

God's eagerness to fulfill the disciples' requests in prayer would have been consistent with the sort of relationship the *Khasidim* enjoyed, but would not have been expected by the average Jew in the street, nor by priests, nor scribes, nor even by most Rabbis.

Jesus was clearly trying to pass His closeness to God along to His disciples. He had established as their goal that they reflect the character of God accurately. He had supplied the example of Abram's devotion, showing them how they needed to grab onto YHWH as the source of all good things and renounce relying on anything else. When He inserted "Ask and you will receive" into His discussion of their training, it appears that His point was that they needed to be praying to become like Him—and that if they did pray that way, they should expect it to come to pass, because in the end it was God who was training them.

Jesus told His students to expect God to answer their prayers "Yes" because it's His nature and His pleasure to do so. In all of Jesus' instruction about prayer, the great desire of God the Father was that His children experience His goodness that occurs everywhere in His kingdom.

This paragraph, similar in Matthew's and Luke's gospel, expresses the heart of His teaching:

> Ask, and it will be given to you; seek, and you will find; knock, and it will be opened to you. For everyone who asks receives, and the one who seeks finds, and to the one who knocks it will be opened. Or which one of you, if his son asks him for bread, will give him a stone? Or if he asks for a fish, will give him a serpent? If you then, who are evil, know how to give good gifts to your children, how much more will your Father who is in heaven give good things to those who ask him![13]

Their confidence in His generosity was to enable them to live as though they were independently wealthy, free to be as generous with everybody as Abram had been with the kings of the Jordan valley:

> Fear not, little flock, for it is your Father's good pleasure to give you the kingdom. Sell your possessions, and give to the needy. Provide yourselves with moneybags that do not grow old, with a treasure in the heavens that does not fail, where no thief approaches and no moth destroys. For where your treasure is, there will your heart be also.[14]

Jesus assured them that God does not need to be convinced to give them "the kingdom," He genuinely wants to do it. We have already established that in the Jewish mind "the kingdom" was the place where God meets all needs with His favor. It was only their human weakness that questioned God's good intentions. To

---

[13] Matthew 7:7-11. See also Luke 11:9-13.
[14] Luke 12:32-34. See also Matthew 6:19-21.

God, the matter was already settled, and the answer was "Yes." The matter that was settled included all their needs, but specifically expressed His aim to enable them to represent His kingdom properly.

It all comes from God's liberality, which is His nature. God dresses the flowers, which don't do anything other than stand there, more lavishly than Solomon ever dressed, so we can expect the same, according to the Rabbi. Imitating Him, we should give liberally to others what they need, because God will give us liberally what we need:

> …give, and it will be given to you. Good measure, pressed down, shaken together, running over, will be put into your lap. For with the measure you use it will be measured back to you."[15]

Believers less certain of God's liberality may point out that the passages I've quoted so far in this chapter lay out conditions on which God's goodness is given. In one passage, "God delights to give you the kingdom" is followed immediately by "Sell all you have and give to the poor." In the other, receiving a good measure poured into your lap follows a clear command, "Give." Such believers might add, accurately, that this last passage, Luke 6:38, suggests that God gives His goodness in proportion to the way we give ours.

Thinking this way makes an understandable mistake, but it's a mistake nonetheless. God's goodness is not granted on the condition of our conduct. Rather, His goodness is granted on the condition of our membership in His kingdom, where His goodness is what rules everywhere. Our good conduct is likewise a result of membership in that kingdom. Our good conduct does not produce His liberality; both are the work of God that flow from Him into those who trust Him. Our access to that liberality

---

[15] Luke 6:38

is determined by how closely we decide to draw to Him; but the liberality never changes, only our closeness to it.

This appears to be the pattern regarding prayer in the scriptures as a whole. God reliably answered the requests of those who lived in a trust-filled relationship with Him, men like Moses, David, Elijah, and Daniel in the Old Testament, and men like Jesus and His disciples in the New Testament. Those who don't have that relationship don't experience the same level of response—not because God doesn't like them, nor because God chooses not to respond, but because they have chosen to live their lives far away from the source of goodness.

They are like the Prodigal Son in the parable in Luke 15; they starve, not because their Father is unwilling to feed them, but because they have placed themselves beyond His reach and choose not to ask. The Prodigal received far better than he asked or deserved as soon as he decided to return to his father. The father's willingness to provide for him never changed; only the Prodigal's ability to receive it changed.

To those who have likewise placed themselves out of His reach, God says "Come closer to Me, and then you will get the good things that are available from Me." It may look from the outside as though their repentance produced God's response, but in fact God's liberality never changed; what changed was that they chose to move to where His will was being done.

There are good examples of this point of view in Isaiah's prophecy. My favorites are Isaiah 55:1-2, where God associates "listen carefully to Me" with obtaining bread and drink that satisfy, and Isaiah 59:2, where God points out that it was their sin, not any choice of His, that separated them from Him. This matches the pattern from Eden in Genesis 3:8: it was not God who dove into the bushes to hide when Man sinned, it was Man. God does not hide Himself from us. We hide ourselves from Him, and losing contact with Him, we also move away from His provision and goodness.

To those who are already in His kingdom but do not have what they need, He counsels, simply, "Ask, and keep on asking, and you'll get it." Jesus' main point about prayers in the Sermon on the Mount was that God loves to tell us "Yes."

## Fear

The problem, of course, is that few of us actually believe that.

The near-automatic caution that we all feel when we are told to expect "Yes" from God is the very thing that Rabbi Jesus was addressing in His students—fear. "Wait a minute," we warn ourselves, "we can't just ask for anything. What if I ask for a million dollars? What if I ask for the past to be undone? What if I ask that Grandma not die, and then she does?" "Life is full of setbacks," we counsel ourselves sagely. "You can't always get what you want."

Of course, what Jesus was talking about specifically was praying to become like the Father. That's why He said it was the Father's pleasure to give them "the kingdom,"[16] and that if human fathers knew how to give good gifts then God was far more willing to give "the Holy Spirit" to those who ask Him.[17] But Jesus was also talking indirectly about asking God for other things, things that we need or want, and His principles were the same for those things.

We're afraid for two reasons. First, we know what is inside ourselves. When we hear "God will give you whatever you ask," we automatically think of what we really want—and some of those things are wicked, greedy, self-centered, or infantile. We're sure that He will despise us for wanting these things; after all, we despise ourselves for wanting them. Our attitudes are those of guilty children facing a stern and angry father, expecting

---

[16] Luke 12:32

[17] Luke 11:13

punishment because we broke the cookie jar, or far worse. (But He does not despise us, and we need not fear.)

Second, we've all experienced disappointment. Some of the things we're asking for are wholesome but we're certain that they are never, ever, *ever* going to happen. We have to shield ourselves, or more to the point, our children from crushing disappointment when our hopes get dashed. In other words, we all feel sure that God will not do as He said He would. (But He will.)

Consistent with our fears, the mass of Protestant believers have been taught that what God really means is that when they pray He will think about it and give them what's good for them, so long as it's also good for Him. This God, though just and all-knowing, is also mean and self-serving; He's not opposed to our having some things so long as it doesn't mess up His plans.

All this fear and caution hides behind wise-sounding teaching: "God answers all prayers. Sometimes He says 'Yes,' sometimes 'No,' and sometimes 'Wait'." I'm still looking for the place in the scriptures where God says that about Himself. I still haven't found it. But it sounds so very wise...

Our fears also result in timid, milquetoast prayers in which we ask for what we want "if it be Your will," because His point of view is so far above ours, as He said in Isaiah 58:8-9. We don't realize that He said this to Israelites who were falling far short of His intent, and that we, His disciples filled with His Spirit, are supposed to learn His ways and understand His thoughts so that we will know His will and be able to pray with confidence. Refusing to believe that He's producing this ability in us, we ask in such a way as to give God an "out," so that He does not have to do as He assured us He would. The Apostle James suggested that we should not expect God to answer such wishy-washy prayers.[18]

---

[18] James 1:5-8

I suspect that a lot of finger-wagging lectures against "the Prosperity Gospel" come from this same set of fears. Certain believers rush to let everyone know that they are not like those wicked fools who imagine that the goodness of God is supposed to make them rich. Some even bring up believers in poorer parts of the world whose prayers for daily bread are literal and who face genuine persecution from a Muslim or Communist majority: "Why don't you tell them how much they're going to prosper…as the ISIL warriors are cutting off their heads?" Most of this agitated talk gets directed against a Straw Man, since few teachers actually teach anything like a "Prosperity Gospel," and many of those who are accused of doing so are simply teaching about how good God is, which is true.

The problem with all of this fear-laden teaching is that it directly combats what Jesus was trying to accomplish with His instruction. Rabbi Jesus' goal was to infuse His *talmidim* with confidence that God was going to give them what they were asking. Far too many teachers set out to remove that confidence so believers won't be disappointed when God does not keep His word.

They need not worry; God will keep His word. He who asks will receive. He who seeks will find. To him who knocks, doors will be opened. This is God's character. Jesus' teaching was clear, and He meant what He said.

Regarding the "What ifs?" at the beginning of this section, I should probably write another book on another day. Real barriers to prayer exist, and we do need to understand them. Only, the most important thing that we need to understand about them is the point that Jesus was emphasizing in the Sermon: that whatever hinders our prayers, "it's not God's will" is almost never the reason. If it were, He would say so.

So if God's will is not the problem, what is?

First of all, we have an enemy. When we pray on earth we are usually battling for contested ground against demonic forces—those that the Apostle called "the rulers...the authorities...the cosmic powers over this present darkness...[and] the spiritual forces of evil in the heavenly places."[19] They do not give up ground on which they're sitting without a fight, and very often when we're praying for anything we're forcing them out. Sometimes they fight back and cause problems for us. It takes time and persistence to overcome the enemy, and situations give way gradually, like athlete's foot responding to medication.

Ironically, it was humans who gave the world over to demonic powers. We forget that God made us humans His regents on Earth,[20] and chose not to intervene except by our agreement.[21] Nearly every complaint that begins "How could God..." and then names some awful thing that humans have to face—bone cancer in children, parents dead in accidents, loved ones raped or murdered—should be answered, "God didn't; Satan did, and we empowered him to do it. It's our fault, not God's."

The fact that we are regents is actually the first reason that we pray. We are not trying to change God's mind or sneak our agenda into His, we are collaborating with Him by His invitation in the management of the planet He gave us. We pray, "Thy will be done," and properly so, but in point of fact God is waiting for us to tell Him our will so that He can do it for us. That's the order He set up on our planet, and He is especially eager to hear requests from the sons and daughters of His kingdom who have grown up enough to rule from His heart.

---

[19] Ephesians 6:12b

[20] "Regent" is defined by Webster's Dictionary as "a person who governs a kingdom in the minority, absence, or disability of the sovereign." We humans are physically present on Earth in a way that God is not, so we act as His regents.

[21] This is another book-length topic for another day. The biblical basis is stated most directly in Psalm 115:16, but there's a lot more that needs to be said about it. The actual grant of regency to humanity occurs in Genesis 1:26-28.

Second, God paints on the canvas of time. He invented time, and usually He works within it. If we pray once, see nothing happen right away, and then give up praying, we may be giving up on something for which we ought to be battling with a longer view. Some tasks might take weeks, months, years, or decades to achieve. Some, like the evangelization of a nation, could take centuries. Some things, like death, will only yield at the end of the age.[22]

It's not very often that He answers some request of ours instantly when He can grant it within the ordinary, time-bound construct of our world. Sometimes He does something instantly, but it's hard to predict when that is going to happen.

When the children are asking that Grandma not die, the answer from God is that eventually, all death will be reversed; He's already accomplished that on the cross, and we have only to wait for it. Moreover, if we'd started praying for Grandma ten years earlier (ironically before the grandkids were born, perhaps), it's likely that she really would stick around longer. But it's a foregone conclusion that Grandma is going to die someday, as all of us will. The final solution for that has already been achieved, but the result comes later. Time is a factor.

Third, I need to add the Apostle Paul's warning about the object of the liberty that we have in the Messiah: "For you were called to freedom, brothers. Only do not use your freedom as an opportunity for the flesh, but through love serve one another."[23] Jesus simply assumed obedience to the rest of His instruction when He explained how God responds to us. Again, the Father is not answering our prayers because we obey, He's answering them because it's His nature; but we're expected to restrain ourselves by our obedience to His nature, too.

---

[22] I Corinthians 15:26
[23] Galatians 5:13

All that said, it is equally true that what we do not ask for, we probably will never receive. I used to teach my own children, "If you don't ask, the answer is automatically 'No.' If you ever want to get to 'Yes,' the only way to get there is to ask." God says the same to His children.

To look at the world and accept its limits as "just the way things are" is to consign ourselves never to see the power of God. What Jesus recommends to us is a different attitude, one which far too few Christians ever dare to adopt: if we find the audacity to ask persistently for what cannot be, then it can be after all. "It is your Father's good pleasure to give you the kingdom." The limits are not what seems possible to human eyes, but rather what we dare to ask God to accomplish for us. We should pray big prayers.

Jesus was not teaching rules, He was teaching attitudes. He was not saying "pray this way and it will work every time." He was saying "Here's what God, your Father, is like." And what we're supposed to take from it is not "seven steps to making sure that your prayers are answered," it's an enjoyable relationship with a smart, fun Dad (who also happens to rule heaven and earth) who genuinely enjoys our company and will respond to our needs and wants out of His goodness and vast supply because He loves doing that. Meanwhile, we can also enjoy collaborating with Dad in His exercise of ruling the universe, because that's what He's raising us up to do.

## A Parable About *Khutzpah*

Jesus tells a *midrash* in Luke's version of this section of the Sermon that illustrates the attitude He recommends. It's so outlandish that many interpreters get the wrong idea entirely.

> And he said to them, "Which of you who has a friend will go to him at midnight and say to him, 'Friend, lend me three loaves, for a friend of mine has arrived on a journey, and I have nothing to set before him'; and he will answer from

within, 'Do not bother me; the door is now shut, and my children are with me in bed. I cannot get up and give you anything'? I tell you, though he will not get up and give him anything because he is his friend, yet because of his impudence he will rise and give him whatever he needs. And I tell you, ask, and it will be given to you; seek, and you will find; knock, and it will be opened to you.[24]

In the Ancient Near East, hospitality was an obligation, not just for individuals but for entire towns and regions. If a person asked for hospitality and was refused, shame fell on the entire town where the person had been refused. So a person asking for bread to set before a traveler did not expect to be refused. The element of this story that Jesus was using to convey His point was the fact that the person was asking at midnight, when people were expected to be asleep.

Typical interpretations of this parable go wrong in two directions. The first misreads the exchange between the sleeping man and his friend at the door and concludes that God wants us to pester Him until He gives in to us. To English readers it does look as though that's what He's saying, but if that were correct it would directly contradict Matthew 6:7-8 and Matthew 6:32, where Jesus assured His students that they don't have to pester their Father because He knows what they need before they ask.

We can resolve that conflict if we just rearrange a Greek sentence in Luke.[25] When the account says in Luke 11:7 that the friend answers "from within," apparently the word order suggests that "within" modifies "house," with the friend calling out to the man at the door from inside the house. However, the word used at that

---

[24] Luke 11:5-9

[25] I found this explanation in a blog posted by a church in central California. The author appears to be correct about the common use of the Greek word "esothen" in the New Testament. The source is https://www.ivchristiancenter.com/2009/09/chutzpah-jesus-word-for-faith-revised.html.

point (ἔσωθεν, "esothen") usually means what a person says within himself. For example, Matthew 7:15 speaks of false prophets who come dressed as sheep but "inwardly ('esothen') are ravenous wolves." That actually fits this situation far better. Nobody lying in bed at midnight is going to have a shouted conversation with the person knocking at his door. If he did, he would wake up everybody else in the house—and in this case, an ordinary house in the Levant, most likely the entire family is sleeping in the same bed. No, upon hearing a knock at his door at midnight the man would drag himself out of bed and stumble silently to the door, muttering "within himself" about what sort of idiot would be knocking at his door at midnight.

Jesus' point was, "The man asking for bread did not get bread because he was asking a friend, he got bread because he had the nerve to knock on his door at midnight." He was encouraging similar nerve when approaching God. There was no pestering involved.

The second, common error keys on the word "impudence" (ἀναίδεια, "anaideia," which means "shamelessness"). Interpreters couple that word with a "Paul on steroids" interpretation of how wicked we all are from Romans 3:10-18,[26] and conclude that what Jesus was saying was that God is

---

[26] In Romans 3:10-18, the Apostle Paul cited a number of passages from the Psalms and one from Isaiah all speaking of how wicked somebody—or everybody—is, and most interpreters take him to mean that all humans are sunk deep in sin. I'm pretty sure, though, that that's a misreading of Paul's intent, and that his actual point was that being a Jew and knowing the Law is no guarantee that a person is righteous and pleases God (since all these quotes were about Jews). My support for that reading comes from Romans 2, in which Paul actually said "Being Jewish does not guarantee anything," and where he seemed to accept that some humans among both Jews and Gentiles will be judged righteous on the last day. See Romans 2:1-16, especially Romans 2:6, 10, and 13. That would have been the normal Jewish understanding. "No human will be judged righteous by God, and we all deserve hell" is simply unheard-of in Jewish thinking. But Paul does go on to say that all humans need redemption in the Messiah.

displaying His enormous grace even to pay the slightest attention to our prayers, since we are such wicked sinners.

They go down that road because the word translated "impudence" occurs nowhere else in the New Testament, but it did occur in other Greek literature, and what it described was never considered a virtue. Quite the contrary, in fact; "shamelessness" was considered a very serious vice, one displayed by criminals and other evil men.

I understand feeling some discomfort with Jesus counseling "shamelessness," but if that reading were correct it would directly contradict the rest of Jesus' teaching about how the Father delights in meeting our needs.

Interestingly, though, modern Jewish usage contains a virtually identical word in Yiddish that is also a vice—except when it isn't. The word is *"khutzpah,"* and lots of non-Jewish Americans are familiar with it.

An apocryphal Jewish story illustrates *khutzpah* by describing a young person who murders his own parents but then pleads for mercy from the judge because he's an orphan. That's shameless, alright. Yet there are plenty of instances where *khutzpah* is used to mean something positive; it means the sort of brashness or aggressiveness that pushes aside convention and fear and gets things done.

For example, I love to coach teenage musicians to play in worship bands. One of the common problems one faces with teenage musicians is that when they have to play alongside adults, they tend to hide like little mice—they play softly so they can't be heard, and they're afraid to try anything interesting lest they be smacked down by the grown-ups. I have to encourage them to play with *khutzpah*—that is, to set aside their fear of doing the wrong thing and instead to be bold and to try out whatever seems right to them. That way, they can contribute to the music. If they make errors it makes little difference and they can be corrected gently, but they make no progress if they can't be heard.

I think that Jesus was after something similar here. He was saying that His students should approach God, the Father, with audacity, not hide behind modesty and fail to ask for what they want. He was encouraging them to be bold because they would certainly get what they were asking for.

In all His instruction about prayer, Jesus encouraged His students to keep in mind God's liberal character, His delight in fulfilling their requests. We also should keep that in mind. We should ask boldly, and we should expect confidently to receive what we have asked. God is not a vending machine, but He does love to give us what we ask, and if for some reason He can't, He'll let us know.

Jesus was not changing the order of Jewish prayer by much, but He was changing the attitude of prayer dramatically. Jesus' prayer was not a religious observance, it was a conversation with a listening Father carried on in confidence that He would give them what they were asking.

# Chapter 9: The School of Humility

Outline of the Sermon on the Mount
Subject: Life in the Kingdom of God

I. God wants you to model His character...    Matthew 5
     A. Ordinary believers are holy    (5:3-12)
     B. Your job is to demonstrate God's character    (5:13-16)
     C. The scriptures are your guide    (5:17-20)
     D. God's character is your standard
         1. Hold relationships in highest esteem    (5:21-26)
         2. Keep your desires ordinate    (5:27-30)
         3. Speak truth at all times    (5:31-37)
         4. Do good to all, not evil    (5:38-48)

II. ...so give Him your whole-hearted devotion...    Matthew 6-7:2
     A. Serve God, not reputation    (6:1-18)
     B. Serve God, not wealth    (6:19-24)
     C. Serve God, not self    (6:25-7:2)

III. ...and He will produce His character in you.    Matthew 7:3-27
     A. Stay humble    (7:3-6)
     B. Pray for God's help    (7:7-12)
     C. Be diligent    (7:13-14)
     D. Stick to the Master's training    (7:15-23)
     E. He will make you unshakable    (7:24-27)

In the last leg of His sermon Jesus explained important principles for students eager to become like their masters. He did not have to convince anybody to seek out masters to teach them; that was already part of the culture and would have been taken for granted. Jesus was teaching that God would reproduce His character in those who devoted themselves to Him in order that they might represent Him accurately to the nations. Consistent with Judaism, though, He expected that God would use human teachers to do it.

## Talmidim

*Talmud* describes the basic pattern for the education of Jewish children:

> At five years old [one is fit] for the Scripture, at ten years the *Mishna* (oral Torah, interpretations) at thirteen for the fulfilling of the commandments, at fifteen the *Talmud* (making Rabbinic interpretations), at eighteen the bride-chamber, at twenty pursuing a vocation, at thirty for authority (able to teach others).[1]

This pattern was followed during Jesus' day. Starting around the age of four or five, children would learn the Torah at the *beth sefer* ("house of the book") attached to their local synagogue until they were ten or twelve. There was a lot of memorizing, as Torah scrolls were very expensive, but students sometimes had small scrolls containing individual prayers or key segments of text. It was an honored goal to memorize the entire Torah while in *beth sefer*, and some of the students achieved it. Girls also attended *beth sefer*; they were expected to memorize Deuteronomy, Psalms, and Proverbs. At the completion of *beth sefer*, boys who had succeeded at memorizing the Torah would be permitted to perform the sacrifice of the Passover lamb for their family at the next Passover in Jerusalem. It seems likely that this is what Jesus was doing in Jerusalem when he was twelve.[2]

After finishing *beth sefer*, children would go back to their families to learn the family business and engage in the ordinary business of life, but more promising students would at the same time continue to learn the rest of *Tanakh* and the Oral Law at *beth hamidrash* ("house of study" or "house of homily"). This they would continue until the age of eighteen or twenty if they

---

[1] Tractate *Avot* 5.21, *The Mishnah*, Herbert Danby, ed., Oxford University Press, Oxford, 1985.

[2] This description comes mostly from Vander Laan, op. cit. Jesus visiting Jerusalem as a 12-year-old is from Luke 2:41-52

continued to show promise. It was not uncommon for students finishing *beth hamidrash* to have memorized, not just the entire *Tanakh*, but also many common interpretations from the Rabbis.

The ordained Rabbis were the heroes of Jewish culture, the "rock stars" to whose fame and piety all Jewish boys aspired. The very few, very best students could apply to a well-established Rabbi during their teen years to become one of his *talmidim*. The Rabbi had to be one who had received *s'mikhah*.[3] The goal of the *talmid* was not just to know what the Rabbi knew, but to become like his Rabbi in every way; it was a life-altering commitment. For that reason, the *talmidim* would follow the Rabbi wherever he went, crowded around him like groupies, hanging on his every word.

Westerners find this hard to picture. We go to school to learn information. That's the modern way, which we inherited from the Greeks and from Christian clerics in the Middle Ages, and it's been modified as recently as the 1970s to avoid sectarian bias in public education; we've leached all the character formation out of our education. But Jews, though interested in information, were more interested in passing along character, so among the Jews of Jesus' day the great Rabbis looked for students in whom they could reproduce themselves. The students they accepted had to have the information down cold, but that was just the starting point; they would accept students who already knew the Law, the prophets, and the *midrash* of the Rabbis, and spend the next several years turning those students into copies of themselves.

This gets expressed in Jesus' observation from Luke's version of this section of the sermon,

> "A disciple is not above his teacher, but everyone when he is fully trained will be like his teacher."[4]

---

[3] I discussed *s'mikhah* back in chapter six, remember?

[4] Luke 6:40. See also Matthew 10:24-25.

Later on a disciple might surpass his teacher, but while in the process of discipleship his goal was to become just like him.

These commitments probably came with dire warnings about their seriousness, like that which Jesus issued in Luke 14:25-33: "If anyone comes to me and does not hate his own father and mother and wife and children and brothers and sisters, yes, and even his own life, he cannot be my disciple." Most students were probably turned away; the Rabbi had to consider the student's potential and his willingness to commit himself totally to the process.

Boys who were good enough students to merit commitment to a Rabbi would begin their training with him during their teen years. Most of them would not marry until they were around twenty, and when they did marry they would generally marry a girl who was only recently old enough to bear children. That's why there's so much talk of widows in the Bible but very little talk of widowers; since men married younger women, the men tended to die first.

Most girls were expected to marry once they were nubile, and were generally passed over for further education once they finished *beth sefer*. However, the picture of Mary sitting at Jesus' feet[5] suggests that Rabbi Jesus may have accepted *talmidot* (female students); to "sit at the feet" of a Rabbi usually expressed a student-teacher relationship with that Rabbi.

Jesus took the unusual step of selecting for Himself the students that He wanted to follow Him, not waiting for them to apply to Him. This was nearly unheard-of.

Notice that when Jesus called Peter, Andrew, James, and John, they were working with their fathers, fishing.[6] This might mean

---

[5] Luke 10:39

[6] Matthew 4:21-22, Mark 1:16-20, Luke 5:1-10. Peter's and Andrew's father was not mentioned, but James and John were partners with them per Luke

that all of them had been passed over for further education. A Rabbi with *s'mikhah* inviting them to become His disciples would have been an amazing opportunity, something like a modern student being offered a full scholarship to Stanford University out of the blue after he had already decided to end his schooling and work at Dad's store. There's no mystery why these young men might have left their parents in the boats; they were being offered the opportunity of a lifetime, education with an ordained Rabbi. Of course the parents would have encouraged them, "Go! Go!", and would have blessed their good fortune.

Because Peter was also apparently married,[7] it's likely that he was twenty or maybe older when Jesus called him. We find support for this from the passage where it appeared that only he and Jesus had to pay the two-drachma temple tax;[8] that tax applied only after the age of twenty.[9] This also may explain why Peter did most of the talking among the disciples and appeared to be their leader. He was probably the oldest by a few years at an age where a few years' difference means a lot.

Once under the careful eye of an authoritative Rabbi, students were strongly encouraged to study in pairs.[10] Many Rabbis in *Gemara* emphasized this practice of seeking out a *khaver* ("partner" or "friend"). Rabbi Yehoshuah ben Perakhiah told students, "Make for yourself a mentor, acquire for yourself a friend, and judge every person as meritorious."[11] *Gemara* quoted

---

5:10, and their father was with them. At a guess, the disciples' fathers may have been partners, too, and then possibly Peter's and Andrew's father passed on.

[7] Matthew 8:14 mentions Peter's mother-in-law.

[8] Matthew 17:24-27

[9] Exodus 30:13-14

[10] Much as I hate to admit it, I took some of this information from Wikipedia. See https://en.wikipedia.org/wiki/Chavrusa. See also https://www.myjewishlearning.com/article/havruta-learning-in-pairs/.

[11] *Talmud*, Tractate *Avot* 1.6. Notice how "judge every person as meritorious" fits with Jesus' warning in this same context, "With the judgment you

in Tractate *Berakhot* 63b says "...Torah is only acquired through study in a group," and adds "those who study alone grow foolish" along with "a sword is upon [those] who sit alone and study Torah." *Gemara* in Tractate *Taanit* 7a quotes Rabbi Khama ben Khanina expounding on Proverbs 27:17 ("Iron sharpens iron...") by saying "...when Torah scholars study together, they sharpen one another in *halakha*." *Khavruta*, the habit of studying in pairs, continues to this day, although Reformed Jews have expanded the practice to use larger groups. This possibly explains why the gospels list Jesus' disciples in pairs,[12] and possibly also why He sent them out in pairs.[13]

## Student Pitfalls

Jesus advised His students to follow the common Jewish model of instruction. That God the Father was to be involved is clear from Jesus' teaching about prayer that He inserted in the middle of His comments about learning; "Ask and you will receive" in this context has to taken as "pray constantly to become like the Rabbi;" and given what I wrote in the last chapter, they were to pray expecting God to do as they asked. But the rest of the teaching in chapter 7 warns the students to be careful to do the right things and avoid dangerous pitfalls in their quest to become Rabbis themselves.

The heavy impact of their choices shows up in the warning that Jesus issued at the heart of the teaching:

> Enter by the narrow gate. For the gate is wide and the way is easy that leads to destruction, and those who enter by it are

---

pronounce you will be judged." (Matthew 7:2)

[12] Matthew 10:2-4, Luke 6:12-16. Mark 3:14-19, being the least Jewish of the gospels, lists them individually.

[13] Luke 10:1. Matthew 10, after listing the Twelve in pairs, says "These Twelve Jesus sent out..." (verse 5). Traditionally this gets interpreted to mean that He sent them in pairs, although the text does not say that directly.

many. For the gate is narrow and the way is hard that leads to life, and those who find it are few.[14]

The warning points out how serious it was that they pursue this education, not just with completely devoted hearts, but with eyes wide open, watching for obstacles. There were apparently plenty of ways that mistakes could ruin the outcome. So Jesus taught them to cooperate with God by devoting themselves with the right attitude to the right teacher.

Jesus was calling them to humility. A surprising percentage of Jesus' instructions in Matthew 7 warn His *talmidim* not to leave the course of instruction before He told them that they were finished. He knew that they might be tempted to cut short the course of instruction and imagine themselves ready to launch out before He told them that they were ready. He actually told His students when they were ready to take the next step, in John 13-16.

Right out of the blocks, Jesus warned them against one of the most common faults that students suffer during the learning process, one which an Internet acquaintance of mine calls "climbing Mt. Stupid." Known formally as the Dunning-Kruger Effect,[15] "climbing Mt. Stupid" refers to the way that students feel like experts when they first discover some new idea. The "Mt. Stupid" reference comes from the bump in a graph like this:

---

[14] Matthew 7:13-14

[15] Kruger, J. and Dunning, D., "Unskilled and unaware of it: how difficulties in recognizing one's own incompetence lead to inflated self-assessments," *Journal of Personality and Social Psychology*, Dec. 1999(6): 1121-1134.

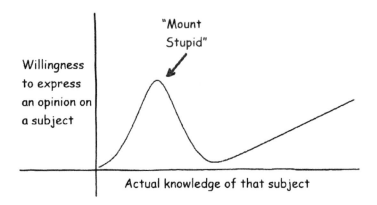

The Internet has acquainted us all with folks—lots and lots of them—who love to tell you what they think about subjects where it's clear that they know next to nothing. This is not just a Christian thing, it's a human thing, but it's painfully common in Christian chat rooms where people with a little bit of Bible knowledge flail angrily at each other over the meaning of some passage or other.

Of course, the Internet has also put a lot of us in touch with our own willingness to do this—or am I the only one who's discovered this?[16] It turns out that when we go from "zero" knowledge to "a little" knowledge, we get a jolt of confidence in our new-found expertise and start explaining it to everyone: "Hey, I know all about this! I read the Wikipedia article!" This goes on until we learn more and find out how it's really a lot more complicated than we first thought. Sometimes it goes on until we run into somebody who really knows the subject and makes us look foolish. Or sometimes it never stops, and we just continue in

---

[16] I suppose that real *Talmud* scholars reading this book might say that I launched the entire book from atop Mt. Stupid, since I'm no *Talmud* scholar. I welcome whatever corrections they care to suggest, though I reserve the right to decide for myself whether what they're saying is accurate and/or relevant to my topic.

our blissful self-delusion. In the best case, we eventually grow out of it.

Jesus described this effect wryly as "a blind man leading a blind man,"[17] and taught His students that when they treat their fellow-students like that they're really trying to "remove a speck from their brother's eye when they have a plank in their own eye."[18] As teacher He had the presence of mind to warn His students how they were going to feel, in Matthew's version adding it immediately after warning them not to judge each other harshly. He had to point it out several more times before He went to the cross; humans being who we are, it's never an idle warning.[19]

This apparently is why Rabbi Yehoshuah ben Perakhiah, advising students how to avoid distractions that would draw them away from Torah and lead them to *Geihinem* ("destruction," denoting a garbage heap outside Jerusalem), told them "Make for yourself a mentor, acquire for yourself a friend, and judge every person as meritorious."[20] Apparently the Jewish sages also recognized that a proper attitude toward instruction required that the student refrain from judging other students.

It's tempting to say that Jesus was teaching them how to pick a teacher; but since they were already His disciples, they did not really need that lesson. In any case a beginner is not usually in a position to know when the person aiming to teach him is actually dangerously ignorant—an excellent reason for any of us to pray seriously and to rely on God when deciding to whom we should listen. Jesus was warning His students not to bully other students with their oh-so-great knowledge until they had become enough like their Teacher to do the job properly.

---

[17] Luke 6:39

[18] Matthew 7:3-5, Luke 6:41-42

[19] See, for example, Matthew 16:21-23, Mark 9:33-37, Luke 9:46-48, Luke 14:7-11, Luke 22:24-27.

[20] *Talmud*, Tractate *Avot* 1.6.

The tendency for students gaining new knowledge to repeat what they've learned probably had something to do with Jesus' next warning, which was that they should choose carefully to whom they repeat their knowledge:

> Do not give dogs what is holy, and do not throw your pearls before pigs, lest they trample them underfoot and turn to attack you.[21]

Of course, this means that the students needed to make an assessment of the character of the people with whom they were speaking. Sometimes you can't do that until you've actually started talking and gotten a reaction. They had to be aware at all times and take nobody for granted.

Jesus was deliberate which animals He used in His analogies. He always used animals to illustrate specific characteristics for which those animals were known.

The dogs He was talking about were not pets. Dogs in the Middle East were wild and traveled in packs, and sometimes they were dangerous. They were also carrion animals: the Old Testament often spoke of dogs eating corpses.[22] The word Jesus used here for dogs was κύων, "kyon"; the same word is used of unclean human beings in Philippians 3:2 and Revelation 22:15, and the Psalmist compared a pack of evil men to dogs in Psalm 22:16.

By contrast, we hear Jesus talking about pets in Matthew 15:21-28 and its parallel in Mark 7:24-30, where He told a Canaanite woman that "It is not right to take the children's bread and throw it to the dogs." There, Jesus used the word κυνάριον, "kynarion," which is diminutive, a cute, little dog. That would have been a pet, which is why the dog might have been in the house with the children eating dinner. Notice that Jesus was talking about pet

---

[21] Matthew 7:6

[22] See, for example, Exodus 22:31, I Kings 14:11, I Kings 21:19, II Kings 9:36, and there are others.

dogs to a Gentile; Jewish families rarely kept dogs as pets, though it was not forbidden.

Jewish farmers did not raise pigs since they had little use for them. Jews had no law against using pigskin for, say, sandals, but it hardly paid to raise pigs since they could not eat their meat. And while pigs are mostly docile, they tend to be bad-tempered, and wild pigs are dangerous.

What the *talmidim* were not to give to dogs or pigs were "what is holy" and "pearls." Pearls were incredibly valuable, and of course holy things were not for ordinary use. Jesus' point was it was useless and dangerous to try to get certain, worthless types of people to accept worthwhile ideas from God's true law.

He may have had something similar in mind when sending out His disciples to do His work for Him.[23] They were apparently not to waste time trying to convince people in towns that did not receive them well; He said, "...when you leave that town shake off the dust from your feet as a testimony against them."[24] It does not actually say that they were to cut short their time in those towns that did not receive them, but it's reasonable to imagine that they might have.

Jesus was also reminding them what sort of students they, themselves, ought to be. Naturally, when He was comparing those who rejected their teaching to dogs or pigs, He was saying just as clearly, "Don't you be a pig, yourself. Show proper regard for your teacher."[25]

After encouraging His students to pray for their own maturity, He repeated this idea as a general proverb:

---

[23] See Matthew 10:14-15, Mark 6:11. Luke 9:5, Luke 10:10-12.

[24] Luke 9:5

[25] I'm reminded of a quote from Aristophanes that I heard in the 2002 film "The Emporer's Club": "Youth ages, immaturity is outgrown, ignorance can be educated, and drunkenness sobered, but stupid lasts forever."

So whatever you wish that others would do to you, do also to them, for this is the Law and the Prophets.[26]

In the context, this might be taken to mean "Be the sort of student that you would like to teach; and when it's your turn to teach, be the sort of teacher from whom you would like to learn." But the more general meaning is there as well.

There was nothing terribly unusual about Jesus teaching the Golden Rule. In the history of the world, similar maxims can be found in the words of Thales, Buddha, Confucius, Maeandrius of Samos, the training of Jain monks, Laotzi, Zoroaster, and a number of others.[27] In Hebrew teaching the lesson could be drawn from the Torah, which teaches "You shall not oppress a sojourner. You know the heart of a sojourner, for you were sojourners in the land of Egypt."[28]

In the *Talmud*, a story contrasting the Rabbis Shammai and Hillel echoes Jesus' assessment of the Golden Rule, "…this is the Law and the Prophets":

> There was another incident involving one gentile who came before Shammai and said to Shammai: Convert me on condition that you teach me the entire Torah while I am standing on one foot. Shammai pushed him away with the builder's cubit in his hand… The same gentile came before Hillel. He converted him and said to him: That which is hateful to you do not do to another; that is the entire Torah, and the rest is its interpretation. Go study.[29]

So the *Talmud* puts "the Golden Rule is the whole Law" in Hillel's mouth. However, we can't say that this Talmudic story

---

[26] Matthew 7:12

[27] See https://charterforcompassion.org/share-the-charter/golden-rule-chronology.

[28] Exodus 23:9

[29] *Talmud*, Tractate *Shabbat* 31a.

predates Jesus. Hillel predated Jesus by almost a hundred years, but Hillel was probably about sixty years old when Shammai was born, and there were very few incidents during which both of them were active Rabbis. The story is most likely *midrash* to contrast the Houses of Hillel and Shammai, so it might have been written after Hillel died. Still, we know that the idea became part of Judaism near the time that Jesus lived.

## False Prophets and False Students

Jesus' next warnings, about false prophets and students who do not do as they have been taught, are not usually combined, but they are remarkably similar. Both of them speak of religious people eager to do things that God did not send them to do. Both types of people get condemned for behaving according to their nature, which is unschooled and unrighteous. Jesus brought them up side by side for a reason.

This section of the Sermon is about how, by devoting themselves to a human teacher, the *talmidim* can come to represent God's own character. These short lessons about false prophets and false students teach that the students cannot become like God unless they hold fast to the character and person of their teacher and remain under His instruction until He sends them out to do His will.

Here's the first part:

> Beware of false prophets, who come to you in sheep's clothing but inwardly are ravenous wolves. You will recognize them by their fruits. Are grapes gathered from thornbushes, or figs from thistles? So, every healthy tree bears good fruit, but the diseased tree bears bad fruit. A healthy tree cannot bear bad fruit, nor can a diseased tree bear good fruit. Every tree that does not bear good fruit is cut down and thrown into the fire. Thus you will recognize them by their fruits.[30]

I hear far too many Protestant teachers speak of false prophets as those who predict something that does not come to pass. They base this on a horrible misreading of Deuteronomy 18:22, in which YHWH assures the people that they need not fear a prophet who predicts things that don't come to pass. Often the intent of the modern, Protestant teachers is to discredit modern, Christian prophets, either because they don't believe that prophecy is a valid gift for the modern Church, or because they do believe that it's a valid gift but they don't like those particular prophets. They are asserting that Christian prophets need to be perfect and cannot make mistakes. This is absurd: it runs contrary to just about everything else we know about God, the Father, Who is patient with us while we learn.

The passage actually speaks to Israel of a Prophet in the same mold as Moses that YHWH will send them. Many interpreters think of this as prophecy of the Messiah, which is possible, but it could just as easily be taken to be YHWH's pattern for the prophets He would send to Israel to keep them on track. In that context, YHWH says:

> But the prophet who presumes to speak a word in my name that I have not commanded him to speak, or who speaks in the name of other gods, that same prophet shall die.[31]

The proper definition of a false prophet appears in that verse. A false prophet is one who speaks in God's name, claiming God's authority, but who is not in fact carrying a message from God. This is a much deeper sin than merely making a mistake and mixing God's revelation with one's own opinion in immature fashion. It involves presumption and arrogance.

A second definition appears in that verse, and it's similar: a false prophet is one who speaks in the name of some god other than YHWH. A useful summary appears in Jeremiah's prophecy, in

---

[30] Matthew 7:15-20
[31] Deuteronomy 18:20

which YHWH says of the prophets of Jerusalem, "I did not send the prophets, yet they ran."[32] And He further condemns them, in that passage in Jeremiah, for prophesying in the name of Ba'al, committing adultery, living in lies, and encouraging those who commit evil acts.

God's displeasure with those who claim His authority where He has not granted it appears in the third of the Ten Commandments:

> You shall not take the name of the Lord your God in vain, for the Lord will not hold him guiltless who takes his name in vain.[33]

I mentioned earlier that refraining from using the word "God" is not a useful way to avoid violating the third commandment.[34] This is why. God is not so much concerned about whether we say "God" or not, He is concerned that we not go around telling others that we have God's authority when we do not. Whether we actually use His name or not while manipulating others hardly matters; if we're posturing as divinely authoritative when we're not, we're wrong, even if we avoid using the word "God." It's not about the word, it's about the abuse of authority.

I get irked when I hear folks talking about the third commandment as though it's just another way of saying "Don't cuss." That trivializes the command. Most "cuss words" have nothing to do with YHWH's name, so this cannot be about "cussing." And while it might be a bad thing to shout Jesus' name when you accidentally slam your thumb with a hammer, that's a flea bite compared to what YHWH really warned them against.

The Father cares generally that people understand the difference between what is holy and what is common; but what really fries

---

[32] Jeremiah 23:21

[33] Exodus 20:7

[34] I said it in note four of chapter three.

His gizzards is when people claim His authority falsely and use it to manipulate others to their own advantage or personal power. That ruins YHWH's name, causing people to reject true messengers and driving them away from His presence. People watch false messengers of the gospel manipulate others to their advantage, using God's name as their authority, and then those people spend the rest of their lives refusing to attend church because in their minds the gospel has become associated with selfish manipulation.

Combining my comments about Matthew 7:1-2, "Don't judge," from chapter seven in this book, with my comments about "Mt. Stupid" at the beginning of this chapter, and both with this observation about how God reacts to those who use His authority without His permission, yields a sober warning against our taking our own interpretations of certain passages from scripture too seriously and using them to condemn other believers. If we take for ourselves the right to judge others by applying things that we know imperfectly (and, let's face it, that's just about everything), we are flirting with taking God's name in vain. He has not sent us to condemn but rather to save.[35] Jesus had the presence of mind to warn His students how a little bit of knowledge might make them eager to judge, and surely God is patient with the mistakes of the immature as they grow; but we should be cautious in our immaturity and refrain from judging, lest God find us guilty: "for the Lord will not hold him guiltless who takes his name in vain." This is probably why Jesus added the warning:

> For with the judgment you pronounce you will be judged, and with the measure you use it will be measured to you.[36]

---

[35] If you want to study this attitude in the scriptures, ponder John 3:17 alongside Jesus' response to the disciples in Luke 9:51-56 when they wanted to imitate Elijah and call down fire from heaven.

[36] Matthew 7:2

In this case, remembering humility to refrain from judging could save us from some uncomfortable judgment, ourselves. Let the wise be warned.

God also cares when He sends servants to warn His people to straighten up, but they fail in their job because they're too corrupt, themselves, to be believed. Both versions make something unwholesome of God's holy name, and cause people to reject that name.

Jesus made the case that such people can be recognized reliably, not when they predict something that doesn't happen, but when they behave according to their unholy nature: "You will recognize them by their fruits."[37] Beneath this claim is the truth that in the end, what people do reflects who they really are on the inside.

> The good person out of the good treasure of his heart produces good, and the evil person out of his evil treasure produces evil, for out of the abundance of the heart his mouth speaks.[38]

Once again, Jesus was precise in choosing to which animal He compared false prophets. He called them "ravenous wolves." They tear people apart, not out of any particular malice toward those people, but simply because it's their nature to feed themselves; they're selfish. But malice or no, people get torn.

Jesus warned that we can't just look at the surface to see the result of their conduct. They come "in sheep's clothing." On the surface they look like anyone else. We have to look at the outcome of their way of life to see what Jesus was calling "fruit."[39]

---

[37] Matthew 7:16

[38] Luke 6:45

[39] I'm echoing Hebrews 13:7, which describes how believers should view sound teachers: "Consider the outcome of their way of life, and imitate their faith." I infer the converse as well; if, as Jesus recommends here in Matthew 7, we consider the outcome of their way of life and see unwholesome things, we

In my lifetime, a number of Protestant teachers who emphasize systematic theology as the real stuff of Christianity have taken Jesus' message about "fruit" and twisted it to be about "sound doctrine." "False doctrine is bad fruit," they insist. They proceed to call anything "false doctrine" that does not conform to their system, and to call those who don't teach what they teach "false teachers."

I acknowledge that any believer holds the right to systematize the truths of the gospel however they find it helpful to do that (with proper regard to the integrity of the text, of course), and to argue forcefully for their interpretation in the marketplace of Christian ideas. However, as soon as they start calling other believers "false teacher" or "false prophet" because those others don't teach their system, they've wandered onto dangerous ground. They could be guilty of the very thing they're denouncing, claiming God's authority to condemn others when He has never sent them to do such a thing.

Such people usually insist that the Apostle Paul instructed them to call out false teachers, but most of the time they've misread a prediction like "some will abandon the faith" to mean a calling like "it's your job to point out who."

The Apostles' concern, like Jesus', was about godly conduct more than it was about systematic theology. Much of the haggling over biblical theology that we hear in Internet forums, probably the Apostle Paul would call "an unhealthy craving for controversy and for quarrels about words,"[40] or "foolish controversies, genealogies, dissensions, and quarrels about the law, [which] are unprofitable and worthless,"[41] or "[quarrelling] about words, which does no good, but only ruins the hearers."[42]

---

should reject them as leaders.

[40] I Timothy 6:4

[41] Titus 3:9

[42] II Timothy 2:14

By contrast, Paul seemed more concerned that we hold fast to the Messiah and to one another, and that we overlook our differences of opinion in favor of the much more important matter of serving one another in love, using the gifts which God has given each of us and keeping ourselves clean from the world's corruption, with proper attention paid to serving the poor.

In nearly every passage in which Paul discussed some false teacher, he mentioned in the context that the point was not correct systematic theology but rather godly behavior. He said such things as "The aim of our charge is love that issues from a pure heart and a good conscience and a sincere faith."[43] He contrasted "irreverent, silly myths" with the command to "train yourself for godliness."[44] He contrasted "[quarrelling] about words" with "'Let everyone who names the name of the Lord depart from iniquity.'"[45] He associated sound doctrine with "Older men are to be sober-minded..." and "Older women likewise are to be reverent in behavior..." and "urge the younger men to be self-controlled," concluding "...the grace of God has appeared, bringing salvation for all people, training us to renounce ungodliness and worldly passions, and to live self-controlled, upright, and godly lives in the present age..."[46]

In other words, what Paul meant by "sound doctrine" is something like "instruction that leads to good behavior." I'm pretty sure that he didn't care a fig for whether we do that following Calvin or Arminius, or John MacArthur or NT Wright for that matter. Go reread I Corinthians 3:1-7 if you doubt me.

In the same manner, to say that Jesus was talking about "sound, systematic theology" when He warned us to examine the fruit of prophets is to twist the meaning of His words beyond

---

[43] I Timothy 1:5

[44] I Timothy 4:7

[45] II Timothy 2:19

[46] Titus 2:1-14

recognition. Don't do that, and don't spend much time learning from those who do that. He was talking about how they behave, and about the effect that that has on those whom they touch.

After that warning, Jesus moved on to talk about students who would not enter the kingdom of heaven because they did not do the will of Jesus' Father:

> Not everyone who says to me, "Lord, Lord," will enter the kingdom of heaven, but the one who does the will of my Father who is in heaven. On that day many will say to me, "Lord, Lord, did we not prophesy in your name, and cast out demons in your name, and do many mighty works in your name?" And then will I declare to them, "I never knew you; depart from me, you workers of lawlessness."[47]

They claim to have been doing works of power in His name, but He disqualifies them on two counts: (1) "I never knew you," and (2) they work lawlessness.

I used to think that this was about developing intimacy with God, and of course that's important. However, what those students will hear "on that day," which would be the day on which the Son judges all men's conduct, is not to be "You never knew Me," but rather "I never knew you." He was speaking from the point of view of the Rabbi who acquired students, trained them, and then sent them out to do His work as fully-trained Rabbis themselves. "I never knew you" means that they were not His students. They may have said that they were acting in His name, but He did not train them and He did not send them, recalling our definition of false prophets, "I did not send them, but they ran anyway."

The notion that they were lawless leads me to apply another animal analogy that Jesus used in a different context. In Matthew 25, where Jesus spoke of judging the nations, He said that He would separate the people "as a shepherd separates the sheep

---

[47] Matthew 7:21-23

from the goats."[48] It's relevant to the idea of lawlessness because of the nature of sheep and goats.

Herding goats reportedly is like herding cats. They don't stick to the herd; they go wherever they feel like going. Sheep, on the other hand, stick together in their herd, and respond to the voice of their shepherd, which in the Middle East is usually a small child. Shepherds can separate a mixed flock by one of them standing to the side and singing, and the sheep from that shepherd's herd will move toward the sound of her voice (assuming a little girl in this case). In fact, I've heard that if one of the shepherd-children dies in an accident, they'll slaughter the whole herd of sheep because they can't be trained to respond to anybody else's voice.

Corresponding to this, Rabbi Jesus called Himself the Good Shepherd and declared, "I know my own and my own know me, just as the Father knows me and I know the Father."[49] But to those who are goats and go their own way, He says "I never knew you; depart from me, you workers of lawlessness."[50]

Naturally, Jesus was not suggesting that His students would be doing anything wrong if they were to "prophesy in [His] name, and cast out demons in [His] name, and do many mighty works in [His] name."[51] He sent them out later to do exactly that. We should still be doing it, and some of us are. The problem with the false students is that they set out to do those things but were not sent to do them. The Rabbi did not know them. They were not His trainees.

The point is that each of us must become His student, pay close attention to His instruction, and not commission ourselves to go where He has not chosen to send us. We should permit Him to

---

[48] Matthew 25:32

[49] John 10:14

[50] Matthew 7:23

[51] Matthew 7:22

train us as He intends, and then go where He sends us when He thinks we're ready.

## On the Rock

Finally, we reach a parable that Jesus told to emphasize the necessity of His instruction to His students. Jesus was not the first Rabbi to teach something like this to His students, nor was He the last. This was not bragging, it was sober recognition of the life-determining seriousness of the things He was teaching, the eternal implications of learning God's ways.

> Everyone then who hears these words of mine and does them will be like a wise man who built his house on the rock. And the rain fell, and the floods came, and the winds blew and beat on that house, but it did not fall, because it had been founded on the rock. And everyone who hears these words of mine and does not do them will be like a foolish man who built his house on the sand. And the rain fell, and the floods came, and the winds blew and beat against that house, and it fell, and great was the fall of it.[52]

Warnings with a similar point appear in the early chapters of Solomon's proverbs. For example:

> Hear, O sons, a father's instruction,
> And be attentive, that you may gain insight,
> For I give you good precepts;
> Do not forsake my teaching…
> Let your heart hold fast my words;
> Keep my commandments, and live.
> Get wisdom; get insight;
> Do not forget, and do not turn away from the words of my
>     mouth.
> Do not forsake her, and she will keep you;
> Love her, and she will guard you…[53]

---

[52] Matthew 7:24-27

...and so on. Jesus' attitude was common for a teacher in the Middle East. In general, constant attention to the precepts taught by a parent or teacher was connected with success in that culture.

Jesus' warning about building on sand may have an interesting source related to dangers in the desert. Those unfamiliar with the desert find it hard to believe how most fatalities happen out there. People can die from thirst, heat stroke, or snakebite, but the largest number of fatalities in the desert happen by drowning.

In rocky deserts like the Negev or the southwest United States, it is common to find narrow canyons with dry stream beds at the bottom. In the western United States such a canyon is called an "arroyo," but in the Middle East it's a "wadi." The streams are usually dry, and they stay dry until there's rain. The rain does not usually fall there in the desert where the wadi is, though; it falls many miles away, in the hills. A person who's down in the wadi can't see or hear the rain. The water, when it shows up, will fill the canyon suddenly in a flash flood, and if a person standing at the bottom of a wadi hears the water coming he's probably a dead man; he's not likely to be able to get out of the wadi before the water reaches him, and he'll be swept away.

Once the rain water has passed on, the sediment left at the bottom of the wadi is mostly sand. By contrast, the walls of the wadi are rock. When a Middle Eastern Rabbi talks about building a house safely on rock versus building it unsafely on sand, it's possible that he's talking about building outside the canyon, up high where the water can't reach, as opposed to building on the sand at the bottom of the wadi. The sand at the bottom may seem like a decent place to put a house, and it will be fine for a while...but the flood will come suddenly and wash everything away.

That's Matthew's version of the story, at any rate. Luke's version also talks about a flood, but specifically mentions digging deep and building a proper foundation.[54] The effect is similar.

---

[53] Proverbs 4:1-2, 4-6

It's a little bit surprising, once you've seen it, to reflect on how much of Matthew 7 is really about sticking with the Teacher until He's finished His work. "The blind leading the blind" is about that; He was warning them against teaching before they were ready. "False prophets" is about that; He was warning them against ministering without being sent, manifesting character flaws that had not been resolved by training. "Not everyone who says to me 'Lord, Lord'" is about that; He was warning them directly to remain His students and not to ignore His lessons. "Building on the rock" is about that; the ones who survived would have put His instruction faithfully into practice. And the summary of them all, "Enter by the narrow gate," is about that.

Just about the only things that did not convey directly the crucial importance of not launching out before the teacher said that they were ready were the brief warnings about throwing pearls in front of pigs, and the instructions to pray. And even those things spoke to being the right sort of student, able to hear and not overly eager to teach.

Jesus had already emphasized to them the crucial importance of whole-hearted devotion to God. Here, Jesus emphasized the second, key characteristic of the student who would prosper under His instruction: humility. They had to be willing to stay rooted in the teacher's instruction for as long as it took to become like Him. And this, some of them did, until He announced that He was leaving and that it was time for them to go out and tell everybody the message.

---

[54] Luke 6:47-49

# Epilogue

Sermon's over. What have we learned?

We've seen Jesus teaching His chosen *talmidim* how to live in the kingdom of God that He was establishing, the kingdom predicted by the Hebrew prophets.

We've seen Jesus using *b'rakhas*, *Tanakh*, and *halakha* to convey to his *talmidim* how they were accurately to demonstrate the character of God and fulfill Israel's role in God's plan to redeem the nations.

We've been reminded that *Tanakh*, the Old Testament, is still authoritative scripture, and have been shown at least one major lesson from it that Jesus used to build into His students the unwavering faith and devotion of Abram, which was to be the starting point for all virtue in God's kingdom.

We've been shown how Jesus encouraged His students through prayer to rely completely on God, their Father, to complete in them the transformation that they needed in order to build His kingdom according to His character.

We heard Jesus calling His disciples to remain in the school of humility until God, their Father, completed His work in them and sent them out to do His works.

And we've seen that, though there was much wisdom already present in Jewish thought, it took the Arm of the Lord to sift through it and focus them on the most important things. Plus, after focusing the wisdom of the sages, Jesus added:

- that there is a higher law of God to which all humans must hold, and the core of that Law is love; and

- that humans can approach God with confidence and expect Him to respond.

Yes, it was a sermon, and yes, it had a consistent theme and a clear message. It clearly made an impression on His *talmidim*. Not only did they note the amazement of everybody who heard, but they remembered the sermon later and were able to write down the contents. Better than that, they took it seriously. They went on to turn the ancient world into the modern world by following His example, and to build a Church that encompasses a third of the world's population and that has taught the nations mercy, compassion, liberty, and productivity. It's a remarkable endorsement of the Sermon on the Mount, one that has been discussed repeatedly in Western literature, as I pointed out way back at the beginning of the book.

So permit me to import another of Jesus' instructions from a slightly different context, and recommend to you all:

"You go, and do likewise."[1] The Church has made progress, but we still have a world to redeem.

---

[1] Luke 10:37b

# Appendix A: A Harmony of the Sermon on the Mount with Luke's Gospel

|  |  |
|---|---|
| Matthew 5:1 Seeing the crowds, he went up on the mountain, and when he sat down, his disciples came to him. 2 And he opened his mouth and taught them, saying: | Luke 6:17 And he came down with them and stood on a level place, with a great crowd of his disciples and a great multitude of people from all Judea and Jerusalem and the seacoast of Tyre and Sidon, 18 who came to hear him and to be healed of their diseases. And those who were troubled with unclean spirits were cured. 19 And all the crowd sought to touch him, for power came out from him and healed them all. 20 And he lifted up his eyes on his disciples, and said: |
| 3 "Blessed are the poor in spirit, for theirs is the kingdom of heaven. 4 "Blessed are those who mourn, for they shall be comforted. 5 "Blessed are the meek, for they shall inherit the earth. 6 "Blessed are those who hunger and thirst for righteousness, for they shall be satisfied. 7 "Blessed are the merciful, for they shall receive mercy. 8 "Blessed are the pure in heart, for they shall see God. 9 "Blessed are the peacemakers, for they shall be called sons of God. 10 "Blessed are those who are persecuted for righteousness' sake, for theirs is the kingdom of heaven. | Luke 6:20b "Blessed are you who are poor, for yours is the kingdom of God. 21 "Blessed are you who are hungry now, for you shall be satisfied. "Blessed are you who weep now, for you shall laugh. |
| 11 "Blessed are you when others revile you and persecute you and utter all kinds of evil against you falsely on my account. 12 Rejoice and be glad, for your reward is great in heaven, for so they persecuted the prophets who were before you. | 22 "Blessed are you when people hate you and when they exclude you and revile you and spurn your name as evil, on account of the Son of Man! 23 Rejoice in that day, and leap for joy, for behold, your reward is great in heaven; for so their fathers did to the prophets. |
|  | 24 "But woe to you who are rich, for you have received your consolation. 25 "Woe to you who are full now, for you shall be hungry. "Woe to you who laugh now, for you shall mourn and weep. 26 "Woe to you, when all people speak well of you, for so their fathers did to the false prophets. |
| Matt 5:13 "You are the salt of the earth, but if salt has lost its taste, how shall its saltiness be restored? It is no longer good for anything except to be thrown out and trampled under | Luke 14:34 "Salt is good, but if salt has lost its taste, how shall its saltiness be restored? 35 It is of no use either for the soil or for the manure pile. It is thrown away. He who has ears to |

| | | |
|---|---|---|
| people's feet. | hear, let him hear." | |
| 14 "You are the light of the world. A city set on a hill cannot be hidden. 15 Nor do people light a lamp and put it under a basket, but on a stand, and it gives light to all in the house. 16 In the same way, let your light shine before others, so that they may see your good works and give glory to your Father who is in heaven. | Luke 11:33 "No one after lighting a lamp puts it in a cellar or under a basket, but on a stand, so that those who enter may see the light. 34 Your eye is the lamp of your body. When your eye is healthy, your whole body is full of light, but when it is bad, your body is full of darkness. 35 Therefore be careful lest the light in you be darkness. 36 If then your whole body is full of light, having no part dark, it will be wholly bright, as when a lamp with its rays gives you light." (See also Matt 6:22-23) | |
| 17 "Do not think that I have come to abolish the Law or the Prophets; I have not come to abolish them but to fulfill them. 18 For truly, I say to you, until heaven and earth pass away, not an iota, not a dot, will pass from the Law until all is accomplished. 19 Therefore whoever relaxes one of the least of these commandments and teaches others to do the same will be called least in the kingdom of heaven, but whoever does them and teaches them will be called great in the kingdom of heaven. 20 For I tell you, unless your righteousness exceeds that of the scribes and Pharisees, you will never enter the kingdom of heaven. | | |
| 21 You have heard that it was said to those of old, 'You shall not murder; and whoever murders will be liable to judgment.' 22 But I say to you that everyone who is angry with his brother will be liable to judgment; whoever insults his brother will be liable to the council; and whoever says, 'You fool!' will be liable to the hell of fire. 23 So if you are offering your gift at the altar and there remember that your brother has something against you, leave your gift there before the altar and go. 24 First be reconciled to your brother, and then come and offer your gift. 25 Come to terms quickly with your accuser while you are going with him to court, lest your accuser hand you over to the judge, and the judge to the guard, and you be put in prison. 26 | | |

|  |  |
|---|---|
| Truly, I say to you, you will never get out until you have paid the last penny. | |
| Matt 5:27 "You have heard that it was said, 'You shall not commit adultery.' 28 But I say to you that everyone who looks at a woman with lustful intent has already committed adultery with her in his heart. 29 If your right eye causes you to sin, tear it out and throw it away. For it is better that you lose one of your members than that your whole body be thrown into hell. 30 And if your right hand causes you to sin, cut it off and throw it away. For it is better that you lose one of your members than that your whole body go into hell. | |
| 31 "It was also said, 'Whoever divorces his wife, let him give her a certificate of divorce.' 32 But I say to you that everyone who divorces his wife, except on the ground of sexual immorality, makes her commit adultery, and whoever marries a divorced woman commits adultery. | |
| 33 "Again you have heard that it was said to those of old, 'You shall not swear falsely, but shall perform to the Lord what you have sworn.' 34 But I say to you, Do not take an oath at all, either by heaven, for it is the throne of God, 35 or by the earth, for it is his footstool, or by Jerusalem, for it is the city of the great King. 36 And do not take an oath by your head, for you cannot make one hair white or black. 37 Let what you say be simply 'Yes' or 'No'; anything more than this comes from evil. | |
| 38 "You have heard that it was said, 'An eye for an eye and a tooth for a tooth.' 39 But I say to you, Do not resist the one who is evil. But if anyone slaps you on the right cheek, turn to him the other also. 40 And if anyone would sue you and take your tunic, let him have your cloak as well. 41 And if anyone forces you to go one mile, go with him two miles. 42 Give to the one who begs from you, and do not refuse the one who would borrow from you. | Luke 6:27 "But I say to you who hear, Love your enemies, do good to those who hate you, 28 bless those who curse you, pray for those who abuse you. 29 To one who strikes you on the cheek, offer the other also, and from one who takes away your cloak do not withhold your tunic either. 30 Give to everyone who begs from you, and from one who takes away your goods do not demand them back 31 And as you wish that others would do to you, do so to them. (See also Matt 7:12.) |

| | |
|---|---|
| Matt 5:43 "You have heard that it was said, 'You shall love your neighbor and hate your enemy.' 44 But I say to you, Love your enemies and pray for those who persecute you, 45 so that you may be sons of your Father who is in heaven. For he makes his sun rise on the evil and on the good, and sends rain on the just and on the unjust. 46 For if you love those who love you, what reward do you have? Do not even the tax collectors do the same? 47 And if you greet only your brothers, what more are you doing than others? Do not even the Gentiles do the same? 48 You therefore must be perfect, as your heavenly Father is perfect. | 32 "If you love those who love you, what benefit is that to you? For even sinners love those who love them. 33 And if you do good to those who do good to you, what benefit is that to you? For even sinners do the same. 34 And if you lend to those from whom you expect to receive, what credit is that to you? Even sinners lend to sinners, to get back the same amount. 35 But love your enemies, and do good, and lend, expecting nothing in return, and your reward will be great, and you will be sons of the Most High, for he is kind to the ungrateful and the evil. 36 Be merciful, even as your Father is merciful. |
| 6:1 "Beware of practicing your righteousness before other people in order to be seen by them, for then you will have no reward from your Father who is in heaven. 2 "Thus, when you give to the needy, sound no trumpet before you, as the hypocrites do in the synagogues and in the streets, that they may be praised by others. Truly, I say to you, they have received their reward. 3 But when you give to the needy, do not let your left hand know what your right hand is doing, 4 so that your giving may be in secret. And your Father who sees in secret will reward you. | |
| 5 "And when you pray, you must not be like the hypocrites. For they love to stand and pray in the synagogues and at the street corners, that they may be seen by others. Truly, I say to you, they have received their reward. 6 But when you pray, go into your room and shut the door and pray to your Father who is in secret. And your Father who sees in secret will reward you. | |
| Matt 6:7 "And when you pray, do not heap up empty phrases as the Gentiles do, for they think that they will be heard for | |

| | |
|---|---|
| their many words. 8 Do not be like them, for your Father knows what you need before you ask him. | |
| 9 Pray then like this:<br><br>"Our Father in heaven,<br>hallowed be your name.<br>10 Your kingdom come,<br>your will be done,<br>on earth as it is in heaven.<br>11 Give us this day our daily bread,<br>12 and forgive us our debts,<br>as we also have forgiven our debtors.<br>13 And lead us not into temptation,<br>but deliver us from evil. | Luke 11:1 Now Jesus was praying in a certain place, and when he finished, one of his disciples said to him, "Lord, teach us to pray, as John taught his disciples." 2 And he said to them, "When you pray, say:<br><br>"Father, hallowed be your name.<br>Your kingdom come.<br>3 Give us each day our daily bread,<br>4 and forgive us our sins,<br>for we ourselves forgive everyone who is indebted to us.<br>And lead us not into temptation." |
| 14 For if you forgive others their trespasses, your heavenly Father will also forgive you, 15 but if you do not forgive others their trespasses, neither will your Father forgive your trespasses. | |
| 16 "And when you fast, do not look gloomy like the hypocrites, for they disfigure their faces that their fasting may be seen by others. Truly, I say to you, they have received their reward. 17 But when you fast, anoint your head and wash your face, 18 that your fasting may not be seen by others but by your Father who is in secret. And your Father who sees in secret will reward you. | |
| 19 "Do not lay up for yourselves treasures on earth, where moth and rust destroy and where thieves break in and steal, 20 but lay up for yourselves treasures in heaven, where neither moth nor rust destroys and where thieves do not break in and steal. 21 For where your treasure is, there your heart will be also. | Luke 12:32 "Fear not, little flock, for it is your Father's good pleasure to give you the kingdom. 33 Sell your possessions, and give to the needy. Provide yourselves with moneybags that do not grow old, with a treasure in the heavens that does not fail, where no thief approaches and no moth destroys. 34 For where your treasure is, there will your heart be also. |

|  | |  |
|---|---|---|
| Matt 6:22 "The eye is the lamp of the body. So, if your eye is healthy, your whole body will be full of light, 23 but if your eye is bad, your whole body will be full of darkness. If then the light in you is darkness, how great is the darkness! | | Luke 11:33 "No one after lighting a lamp puts it in a cellar or under a basket, but on a stand, so that those who enter may see the light. 34 Your eye is the lamp of your body. When your eye is healthy, your whole body is full of light, but when it is bad, your body is full of darkness. 35 Therefore be careful lest the light in you be darkness. 36 If then your whole body is full of light, having no part dark, it will be wholly bright, as when a lamp with its rays gives you light." (See also Matt 5:14-15) |
| 24 "No one can serve two masters, for either he will hate the one and love the other, or he will be devoted to the one and despise the other. You cannot serve God and money. | | |
| 25 "Therefore I tell you, do not be anxious about your life, what you will eat or what you will drink, nor about your body, what you will put on. Is not life more than food, and the body more than clothing? 26 Look at the birds of the air: they neither sow nor reap nor gather into barns, and yet your heavenly Father feeds them. Are you not of more value than they? 27 And which of you by being anxious can add a single hour to his span of life? 28 And why are you anxious about clothing? Consider the lilies of the field, how they grow: they neither toil nor spin, 29 yet I tell you, even Solomon in all his glory was not arrayed like one of these. 30 But if God so clothes the grass of the field, which today is alive and tomorrow is thrown into the oven, will he not much more clothe you, O you of little faith? 31 Therefore do not be anxious, saying, 'What shall we eat?' or 'What shall we drink?' or 'What shall we wear?' 32 For the Gentiles seek after all these things, and your heavenly Father knows that you need them all. 33 But seek first the kingdom of God and his righteousness, and all these things will be added to you. | | Luke 12:22 And he said to his disciples, "Therefore I tell you, do not be anxious about your life, what you will eat, nor about your body, what you will put on. 23 For life is more than food, and the body more than clothing. 24 Consider the ravens: they neither sow nor reap, they have neither storehouse nor barn, and yet God feeds them. Of how much more value are you than the birds! 25 And which of you by being anxious can add a single hour to his span of life? 26 If then you are not able to do as small a thing as that, why are you anxious about the rest? 27 Consider the lilies, how they grow: they neither toil nor spin, yet I tell you, even Solomon in all his glory was not arrayed like one of these. 28 But if God so clothes the grass, which is alive in the field today, and tomorrow is thrown into the oven, how much more will he clothe you, O you of little faith! 29 And do not seek what you are to eat and what you are to drink, nor be worried. 30 For all the nations of the world seek after these things, and your Father knows that you need them. 31 Instead, seek his kingdom, and these things will be added to you. |
| Matt 6:34 "Therefore do not be anxious about tomorrow, for tomorrow will be anxious for itself. Sufficient for the day is its | | |

| | |
|---|---|
| own trouble. | |
| 7:1 "Judge not, that you be not judged. 2 For with the judgment you pronounce you will be judged, and with the measure you use it will be measured to you. | Luke 6:37 "Judge not, and you will not be judged; condemn not, and you will not be condemned; forgive, and you will be forgiven; 38 give, and it will be given to you. Good measure, pressed down, shaken together, running over, will be put into your lap. For with the measure you use it will be measured back to you." |
| 3 Why do you see the speck that is in your brother's eye, but do not notice the log that is in your own eye? 4 Or how can you say to your brother, 'Let me take the speck out of your eye,' when there is the log in your own eye? 5 You hypocrite, first take the log out of your own eye, and then you will see clearly to take the speck out of your brother's eye. | Luke 6:39 He also told them a parable: "Can a blind man lead a blind man? Will they not both fall into a pit? 40 A disciple is not above his teacher, but everyone when he is fully trained will be like his teacher. 41 Why do you see the speck that is in your brother's eye, but do not notice the log that is in your own eye? 42 How can you say to your brother, 'Brother, let me take out the speck that is in your eye,' when you yourself do not see the log that is in your own eye? You hypocrite, first take the log out of your own eye, and then you will see clearly to take out the speck that is in your brother's eye. |
| 6 "Do not give dogs what is holy, and do not throw your pearls before pigs, lest they trample them underfoot and turn to attack you. | |
| 7 "Ask, and it will be given to you; seek, and you will find; knock, and it will be opened to you. 8 For everyone who asks receives, and the one who seeks finds, and to the one who knocks it will be opened. 9 Or which one of you, if his son asks him for bread, will give him a stone? 10 Or if he asks for a fish, will give him a serpent? 11 If you then, who are evil, know how to give good gifts to your children, how much more will your Father who is in heaven give good things to those who ask him! | Luke 11:5 And he said to them, "Which of you who has a friend will go to him at midnight and say to him, 'Friend, lend me three loaves, 6 for a friend of mine has arrived on a journey, and I have nothing to set before him'; 7 and he will answer from within, 'Do not bother me; the door is now shut, and my children are with me in bed; I cannot get up and give you anything'? 8 I tell you, though he will not get up and give him anything because he is his friend, yet because of his impudence he will rise and give him whatever he needs. 9 And I tell you, ask, and it will be given to you; seek, and you will |

|  |  |
|---|---|
|  | find; knock, and it will be opened to you. 10 For everyone who asks receives, and the one who seeks finds; and to the one who knocks it will be opened. 11 What father among you, if his son asks for a fish, will instead of a fish give him a serpent; 12 or if he asks for an egg, will give him a scorpion? 13 If you then, who are evil, know how to give good gifts to your children, how much more will the heavenly Father give the Holy Spirit to those who ask him!" |
| Matt 7:12 "So whatever you wish that others would do to you, do also to them, for this is the Law and the Prophets. | Luke 6:31 And as you wish that others would do to you, do so to them. (See also Matt 5:38.) |
| 13 "Enter by the narrow gate. For the gate is wide and the way is easy that leads to destruction, and those who enter by it are many. 14 For the gate is narrow and the way is hard that leads to life, and those who find it are few. |  |
| 15 "Beware of false prophets, who come to you in sheep's clothing but inwardly are ravenous wolves. 16 You will recognize them by their fruits. Are grapes gathered from thornbushes, or figs from thistles? 17 So, every healthy tree bears good fruit, but the diseased tree bears bad fruit. 18 A healthy tree cannot bear bad fruit, nor can a diseased tree bear good fruit. 19 Every tree that does not bear good fruit is cut down and thrown into the fire. 20 Thus you will recognize them by their fruits. | Luke 6:43 "For no good tree bears bad fruit, nor again does a bad tree bear good fruit, 44 for each tree is known by its own fruit. For figs are not gathered from thornbushes, nor are grapes picked from a bramble bush. 45 The good person out of the good treasure of his heart produces good, and the evil person out of his evil treasure produces evil, for out of the abundance of the heart his mouth speaks. |
| 21 "Not everyone who says to me, 'Lord, Lord,' will enter the kingdom of heaven, but the one who does the will of my Father who is in heaven. 22 On that day many will say to me, 'Lord, Lord, did we not prophesy in your name, and cast out demons in your name, and do many mighty works in your name?' 23 And then will I declare to them, 'I never knew you; depart from me, you workers of lawlessness.' | Luke 6:46 "Why do you call me 'Lord, Lord,' and not do what I tell you? |
| Matt 7:24 "Everyone then who hears these words of mine and | Luke 6:47 "Everyone who comes to me and hears my words |

| | |
|---|---|
| does them will be like a wise man who built his house on the rock. 25 And the rain fell, and the floods came, and the winds blew and beat on that house, but it did not fall, because it had been founded on the rock. 26 And everyone who hears these words of mine and does not do them will be like a foolish man who built his house on the sand. 27 And the rain fell, and the floods came, and the winds blew and beat against that house, and it fell, and great was the fall of it." | and does them, I will show you what he is like: 48 he is like a man building a house, who dug deep and laid the foundation on the rock. And when a flood arose, the stream broke against that house and could not shake it, because it had been well built. 49 But the one who hears and does not do them is like a man who built a house on the ground without a foundation. When the stream broke against it, immediately it fell, and the ruin of that house was great." |
| 28 And when Jesus finished these sayings, the crowds were astonished at his teaching, 29 for he was teaching them as one who had authority, and not as their scribes. | |

# Appendix B: From Babylonian Talmud, Tractate Shabbat[*]

## Regulations Regarding Transfer on Sabbath

MISHNA I.: There are two acts constituting transfer of movable things (over the dividing line of adjoining premises, based on biblical statutes). The two acts are, however, increased to four on the inside and to a like amount on the outside of the premises (by the addition of rabbinical statutes). How so? A mendicant stands outside and the master of a house inside. The mendicant passes his hand into the house (through a window or door) and puts something into the hand of the master, or he takes something out of the master's hand and draws it back (toward him). In such a case the mendicant is guilty (of transfer) and the master of the house is free. If the master of the house passes his hand outside and puts a thing into the hand of the mendicant, or takes something out of the mendicant's hand and brings it into the house, the master of the house is culpable and the mendicant is free. If the mendicant extends his hand into the house and the master takes something out of it, or puts something into it which is drawn to the outside by the mendicant, they are both free. If the master of the house extends his hand outside and the mendicant takes something out of it, or puts something into it which is drawn to the inside by the master, they are both free.

GEMARA: We were taught (Shebuoth, IV. 2): "The acts of transfer on the Sabbath are two, respectively four." Why is this teaching here specified as two respectively four on the inside, and two respectively four on the outside, and there no such specification was made? Said R. Papa: Here the special subject of treatment is the Sabbath, and the Mishna enumerated the cases

* http://www.jewishvirtuallibrary.org/tractate-shabbat-chapter-1

which involve guilt and those which do not involve guilt; while there the principal subject of treatment is a different one, and he mentions only the cases that involve guilt, leaving the cases that do not involve guilt untouched. But the cases that involve guilt are those by which acts of transfer are committed, and such are only two? Nay, there are two acts of transfer from within and two from without. But the Mishna says, "Yetziath" (which in a literal sense means transfer from within)? Said R. Ashi: The Tana calls transfer from without by the same term. And for what reason? Because every act of removing a thing from its place is called Yetziah. Said Rabbina: The Mishna also bears out this sense; for it speaks of Yetziath and immediately illustrates its remark by citing a case from without. This bears it out. Rabha, however, says: He (the Tana) speaks about divided premises (whose line of division is crossed), and in this case there are only two (in each of which there may be four acts of transfer).

Said R. Mathna to Abayi: Are there not eight, even twelve (instances of transfer over the line of division)? And he rejoined: Such transfers as involve the obligation of a sin-offering are counted; but those that do not involve such an obligation are not counted.

"*They are both free.*" Was not the act (of transfer) committed by both? Said R. Hyya bar Gamda: The act of removing the thing was committed by the joint efforts of both, and they (the rabbis) said: "It is written in the law, when a person did it"--*i.e.*, when one person commits the act he is culpable, but when an act is committed by the joint efforts of two persons, they are both free.

Rabh questioned Rabbi: If one were laden by his friend with eatables and beverages and carried them outside (of the house), how is the law? Is the removing of his body tantamount to the removing of a thing from its place, and therefore he is culpable, or is it not so?

Said Rabbi to him: He is culpable. And this case is not like the case of removing his hand. Why so? Because (in the latter case) the hand was not at rest, while (in the former) the body (before and after removal) was entirely at rest.

Said Rabbi Hyya to Rabh: Descendant of nobles! Did I not tell thee that when Rabbi is engaged with a certain tract ask him not about a subject (that is treated) in another tract, for he may not have that subject in his mind! And if Rabbi were not a great man thou mightest cause him shame, for he would give thee an answer which might not be right. In this instance, however, he gave thee a correct answer; as we have learned in the following Boraitha: If one was laden with eatables and beverages while it was yet light on the eve of Sabbath, and he carried them outside after dark, he is culpable; for his case is not like that of removing the hand mentioned above.

Abayi said: From all that was said above it is certain to me that the hand of a man (standing on the street) is not treated as public ground. And I also see that (if a man stands on private ground) his hand is not to be treated a-, private ground. Would it be correct, then, to regard the hand as unclaimed ground? If so, would the penalty imposed by the rabbis in such a case, namely, that one should not move his hand (containing a movable thing) back (during the Sabbath day), apply in this case or not?

Come and hear the following Boraitha: If a man has his hand filled with fruit and he extends it outside (of the premises where he stands), one said he is not permitted to draw it back, and another Boraitha says he is allowed to do so. May we not assume that this is their point of dispute: the former holds that the hand is treated as unclaimed ground, and the latter thinks that it is not like unclaimed ground? Nay, it may be that both agree that the hand (as spoken of in our Mishna) is like unclaimed ground, and yet it presents no difficulty. One of the Boraithas treats of a man who had extended his hand unintentionally, and the other one treats of a man who had put forth his hand intentionally. In the former case the rabbis did not fine him, and in the latter case they did. And if you wish, it may be said that they both speak of a case when the act was done unintentionally, and their point of differing is as to the varying premises, whether the hand may be drawn back to the ground where the man stands, or to other (private) ground that adjoins it? As Rabha questioned R. Na'hman: If the hand of a man was filled with fruit, and he extended it outside, may he draw it back to the same ground where he stands? And he answered: He may. (And may he remove his hand) to other (private) ground? Nay. And to the question, "What is the distinction?" he said: If thou wilt measure a whole kur of salt and present me with it, I shall tell thee the answer. In the former case his design was not accomplished; in the latter, however, his design was accomplished (and it is prohibited for fear that it should be repeated).

R. Bibi bar Abayi questioned: If one has put bread into the oven, is he allowed to take it out before (it is baked and) he becomes liable to bring a sin-offering, or not?

Said R. A'ha bar Abayi to Rabhina: What does the questioner mean? Unintentionally and without remembering (that it is Sabbath), then what does the expression "allowed" mean? To whom? He is still not aware of it. On the other hand, if he did it unintentionally and afterward he remembered of the Sabbath, how can he be liable to a sin-offering; did not a Mishna state that the liability to bring such a sacrifice applies only when the failing was begun and accomplished unintentionally? Should it be understood that the act was done intentionally, then it would not involve the liability of a sin-offering, but it would constitute a crime that involved capital punishment.

Said R. Ashi: Say, then, it is a crime that involves capital punishment. R. A'ha, the son of Rabha, taught so plainly. R. Bibi bar Abayi said: If one put bread into the oven, he is allowed to take it out before it may involve a case of capital punishment.

"The mendicant extended his hand," etc. Why is he culpable? (To complete the act) there must be a transfer from a place that is four ells square and a depositing into a place of the same area, and such was not the case here. Said Rabba: Our Mishna is in accordance with R. Aqiba's opinion, who holds that as soon as the air of a place surrounds a thing it is equal to the thing being deposited in that place. But may it not be that depositing does not require four ells, for the reason stated above, but removing does? Said R. Joseph: The teaching of this paragraph agrees (not with the opinion of R. Aqiba), but with that of Rabbi, as we have learned in the following Boraitha:

If one threw an object from one street into the other, and there was a private ground between them, Rabbi declared him culpable, and the sages freed him. Hereupon R. Jehudah in the name of Samuel said: Rabbi declared the man guilty of two offences: one for having removed the thing from its place, and one for having deposited it in another place. Hence in both, the four ells in question are not required.

But with reference to this it was taught that both Rabh and Samuel said that Rabbi's declaration of culpability treated of a case where the private ground (that divided the two streets) was roofed, for the assumption is that a house must be regarded as a solid object that fills out all the space it occupies, but not when it was unroofed?

Therefore said Rabha: (All these views can be dispensed with, as) the hand of a man (because of its value) is considered as a piece of ground four ells square. And so, also, was declared by Rabin, when he came from Palestine, in the name of R. Johanan.

R. Abhin in the name of R. Ila'a, quoting R. Johanan, said: If one threw a thing and it rested in the hands of another man, he is culpable…

(And so on for another 4 pages or so…)

## About the Author

Phil Weingart is a retired IT consultant with many years' experience writing Christian apologetics, politics, and philosophy on the Internet, beginning before "Internet" was a household word. He is a lay teacher at the Bridgewater Vineyard Church in East Bridgewater, MA, and has preached at several churches in the area. He holds a BA in Rhetoric and an MBA emphasizing Information Systems from the University of Pittsburgh. He writes a bi-weekly teaching called "RfMemo" which is available through his web site, www.philweingart.net.

He currently lives in southeast Massachusetts with his wife, Shelly. Shelly also writes and illustrates her own books.

Phil's first book, *He's Greater Than You Know*, was a compilation of his essays taken from Internet forums and assembled to answer the specific questions of a believer having an intellectual crisis. It's available on his web site and Amazon.

# Phil Weingart

**Christianity Can Be Sensible**

Rf | Memo

I write a biweekly email newsletter called "Rf Memo." It's 1000+ words (about 2 pages) of sensible encouragement and information supporting your relationship with Jesus and demonstrating the truth of the Christian faith.

If you'd like to receive it, please visit my web site at

## http://www.philweingart.net

...and fill out the subscription form that's on the side bar. You can also browse the archives of earlier newsletters under the "RF Memos Archive" tab.

Also, look for "Remedial Faith" on facebook. That's mine, too.

Christianity can be sensible...


Phil Weingart

Printed in Great Britain
by Amazon